Most-Used Shorthand Words and Phrases

CLASSIFIED ACCORDING TO THE LESSONS IN
THE GREGG SHORTHAND MANUAL SIMPLIFIED

John Robert Gregg

Louis A. Leslie

Charles E. Zoubek

GREGG PUBLISHING DIVISION

McGraw-Hill Book Company, Inc.

New York   Chicago   San Francisco   Dallas   Toronto   London

MOST-USED SHORTHAND WORDS AND PHRASES

Aug. 1958-RD

Code No. 24542

Shorthand Plates Written by
CHARLES E. ZOUBEK

PUBLISHED BY GREGG PUBLISHING DIVISION
McGraw-Hill Book Company, Inc.
Printed in the United States of America

Printing Statement:

Due to the very old age and scarcity of this book, many of the pages may be hard to read due to the blurring of the original text, possible missing pages, missing text and other issues beyond our control.

Because this is such an important and rare work, we believe it is best to reproduce this book regardless of its original condition.

Thank you for your understanding.

PREFACE

Most-Used Shorthand Words and Phrases contains the short-hand outlines for 3,669 words and 1,696 phrases selected on the basis of usefulness and frequency.

The words were selected from the first 10,000 words in order of frequency of the Horn-Peterson *Basic Vocabulary of Business Letters*. That work contains the 14,834 different words found in a count of 1,500,000 words of business letters chosen from 26 kinds of business. The 3,669 words in *Most-Used Shorthand Words and Phrases* were chosen from the first 10,000 in order of frequency on the basis of the greatest usefulness to the stenographer in the business office. Many of the first 10,000 words in order of frequency are simple derivatives in *-ing, -ed, -s* that the shorthand writer can construct for himself when the primitive form is given. In the rare cases when such derivatives present any stenographic problem, they are given. Thus the 3,669 shorthand outlines in the word list comprise almost all the stenographic value of the 10,000 most frequently used words in business dictation. An Index to the words begins on page 113. For each word listed, there is a reference to the lesson in which the word may first be written.

The 1,696 phrases in this book were selected from the 3,536 different phrases found by one of the authors in a business-letter phrase-frequency count of 250,000 running words of business-letter dictation. Approximately one-third of the phrases (1,445) occurred only once in the 250,000 words and therefore do not appear in the present list. It is interesting to note that the first 100 different phrases in order of frequency, with their repetitions, account for 15,631 of the total of 33,202 phrases occurring in the 250,000 running words of dictation.

The key to good phrasing is simplicity. Of the 3,536 different phrases in the phrase-frequency count, 2,183 contain only two words each.

Chapter I of this book contains 721 words and 326 phrases. Chapter II contains 342 words and 507 phrases. Thus, after completing the first two chapters of the *Gregg Shorthand Manual Simplified,* the learner can write 1,063 of the most useful business words and 833 of the most useful business phrases. The fact that almost exactly half the most useful business phrases may be written after the completion of the first two chapters of the *Manual* emphasizes the simplicity of good phrases.

The shorthand teaching profession owes a great debt to Doctor Horn and to Miss Peterson for their invaluable *Basic Vocabulary of Business Letters.*

The Publishers

CHAPTER I

LESSON 1

A, S-Z, F, V

face		safe		say	
phase		save		vase	

E, N, M

easy		knee		aim	
fee		navy		main	
fees		sane		may	
sea		scene		me	
see		seen		mean	
sees		vain		same	

T, D

ate		stain		deed	
east		stay		feed	
faced		steam		made	
feet		tea		need	
meat		team		saved	
neat		aid		seed	
seat		day		stayed	

1

O, R, L

foe	dear	deal
know	drain	fail
no	drove	feel
note	fair	late
sew	free	lead
snow	freight	leave
so	near	low
stove	rate	mail
stow	road	real
toe	trade	relay
vote	treat	retail
zone	wrote	steal

H

hair	hate	heat
haste	hear	heed

Omission of minor vowels

dealer	heater	notary
Easter	later	phone
even	meter	reader
favor	motor	season
hasten	nearer	total

LESSON 2

S-Z, P, B

days		hope		able	
knows		open		base	
least		paid		better	
means		paper		blame	
niece		pays		boats	
notes		people		brief	
readers		place		labor	
seems		prepare		neighbors	

K, G

broke		cream		game	
came		keys		gave	
claim		sake		girls	
clear		taken		grade	
close		gain		grow	

Sh, Ch, J

shade		chains		age	
shaped		cheaper		changed	
shares		chose		page	
sheep		each		range	
show		reached		storage	

The diphthong *i*

buy		hide		rise	
cried		iron		slight	
drive		light		styles	
dry		might		tire	
dye		night		tried	
files		obliged		type	
height		rely		vital	

LESSON 3

Additional sounds of *a* and dot for *-ing*

add		alarm		aiming	
advice		arm		bearing	
agree		army		casting	
appear		bargain		charming	
arrive		charged		evening	
average		far		grading	
capital		farms		greeting	
fast		harm		heating	
habit		large		leasing	
has		mark		lining	
master		star		making	
sample		starts		trading	

Additional sounds of *e*

bids

bed

church

chickens

check

earn

drill

fellow

firms

familiar

getting

her

given

helped

hurry

him

led

hurt

little

medal

major

middle

pledge

search

river

seller

serve

similar

settle

urge

Upward strokes for *th*

bath

healthy

thickness

birth

lath

thinner

birthday

thick

throat

Phrases

as if

if my

has no

as these

if so

each night

as though

if these

gave me

each case

give me

my dear

each day

has had

so large

has given

has known

so late

has met

has made

so low

Brief forms

a	goes	its	
ago	going	more	
am	good	not	
an	goods	our	
are	he	ours	
at	hour	the	
can	hours	well	
cannot	I	will	
can't	in	wills	
go	it	would	

Phrases

are

are not   here are   these are

at

at least   at the   at these

good

as good   good deal

he

he came	he drove	he goes
he can	he fell	he knows
he can make	he felt	he left
he can't	he gets	he lives

he made	he reaches	he will not
he may	he said	he will say
he needs	he will	he would

I

I am	I guess	I reached
I came	I know	I read
I can	I left	I realize
I cannot	I live	I said
I can see	I make	I say
I drove	I mean	I see
I fear	I met	I will
I feel	I might	I will not
I felt	I need	I will see
I gave	I need not	I would
I get	I notice	I would not
I give	I ran	I wrote

in

| in case | in its | in the |
| in it | in our | in these |

it

| as it | if it | it will |
| as it will | it has | it will not |

the

as the		has the		make the	
ask the		if the		realize the	

not

had not		has not		might not

will, well

as well		well known		will pay
so well		will not		will see

LESSON 4

Short sound of *o*

adopt	crossed	logs
block	dock	loss
blotter	dog	lost
bronze	drop	lot
catalogue	hog	mob
clock	hop	model
co-operate	hospital	moderate
copies	hot	mop
copper	job	observe
cottage	jobber	occur
crop	lobby	occurrence
cross	lock	off

offer	pocket	shop
offset	popular	soft
often	remodeling	spot
oftener	rob	stock
operate	rock	stop
opposite	rod	top

Aw

abroad	brought	jaw
absorb	caught	laws
auto	cause	ought
bought	caused	raw
broad	clause	saw
broadcasting	daughter	talked
broader	draw	taught

Phrases

across the	he saw	I talked
has taught	he talked	I thought
he lost	I saw	off the

Brief forms

be	by	have
before	could	herewith
but	for	his

is	⟩	ship	/	therefore	
of	ᴜ	their	⟋	therein	
put	⟮	there	⟋	which	/
shall	/	thereby		with	

Phrases

be

can be		I will be		might not be	
cannot be		I would be		need be	
can't be		if it will be		need not be	
he can be		in behalf		on behalf	
he will be		it will be		she may be	
he would be		it will not be		will be	
I can be		may be		will not be	
I cannot be		may not be		would be	
I can't be		might be		would not be	

by

by it		by mail		by these	
by its		by the		by which	

could

could be		he could		I could be	
could not		he could not		I could not	
could not be		I could		I could see	

for

for his	for my	for these
for it	for our	for which
for its	for the	for which the
for me	for their	before the

have

can have	I have	I would have
have given	I have had	it will have
have had	I have made	may have
have made	I have not	might have
have not	I have tried	will have
he will have	I may have	will not have
he would have	I will have	would have

is, his

as it is	if it is	is there
he is	in his	it is
he is not	is it	on his
he is the	is not	she is
here is	is the	she is not

of

of his	of our	of their
of it	of ours	of these
of its	of the	of which

shall

I shall	I shall make	shall be
I shall be	I shall not	shall not
I shall have	I shall see	shall not be

there, their

as there	if there will	there may be
as there is	there are	there will
if there are	there is	there will be
if there is	there may	there would be

with

with him	with the	with which
with our	with these	with which the

which

in which	on which the	which may
in which the	which is	which may be
on which	which is the	which means

LESSON 5

The combination *ses*

access	analysis	balances
addresses	arises	bases
advances	assessed	basis
advices	auspices	braces

cases	↗	glasses	⌐	premises	⌐
causes	↗	leases	⌐	presses	⌐
census	↗	lenses	⌐	prices	⌐
chances	↗	losses	⌐	releases	⌐
classes	↗	mattresses	⌐	says	⌐
clauses	↗	necessitate	⌐	services	⌐
closes	↗	necessity	⌐	sister	⌐
courses	↗	notices	⌐	sizes	⌐
criticism	↗	nurses	⌐	sources	⌐
faces	↗	passes	⌐	spaces	⌐
finances	↗	places	⌐	versus	⌐

To in phrases

as to be		to break		to fill	
has to be		to burn		to finance	
is to be		to buy		to finish	
to balance		to change		to fit	
to be		to charge		to fly	
to bear		to check		to follow	
to beat		to face		to have	
to bite		to fall		to jar	
to blame		to farm		to park	
to borrow		to feel		to pass	

to pay		to see		to spare	
to pick		to sell		to speed	
to place		to separate		to spread	
to plan		to serve		to supply	
to play		to serve you		to surprise	
to post		to share		to survey	
to prepare		to shift		to visit	
to preserve		to ship		to which	
to put		to show		to which the	
to say		to slide		to which you	

Strokes for *x*

affix		fixes		taxed	
box		flax		taxes	
boxed		mix		taxicab	
boxes		mixed		text	
fix		mixer		textile	
fixed		tax			

LESSON 6

Circles inside curves
Two curves in the same direction

appeal		bear		built	
barrel		belt		buyer	

cave　　　give　　　park

gift　　　pair　　　spare

At the beginning or end of curves

apply　　　error　　　happy

again　　　gay　　　heavy

arm　　　gray　　　help

art　　　half　　　if

cry　　　happen　　　pay

Straight line and curve joining without angle

accurate　　　dig　　　light

bread　　　flat　　　read

bright　　　gauge　　　rid

cash　　　hosiery　　　plate

cashier　　　jar　　　share

catch　　　jelly　　　shell

chair　　　journal　　　sharp

charge　　　kitchen　　　take

Outside angles
Between straight lines

chain　　　match　　　net

jam　　　met　　　omit

machine　　　metal　　　teacher

Straight line and curve joining with angle

arrange		finish		mile	
bad		fit		milk	
battery		fresh		mill	
benefit		get		oblige	
bid		green		pin	
branch		guide		plain	
bridge		hotel		plan	
campaign		ledger		ran	
cheap		line		reach	
chief		make		shape	
clean		map		telephone	
dark		March		tell	
decline		margin		territory	
deep		marked		tip	
federal		material		tire	
final		merit		type	

Between two curves

back		clearer		factory	
bag		clerk		farm	
baggage		clipping		fell	
beg		draft		file	
cabinet		driver		fill	

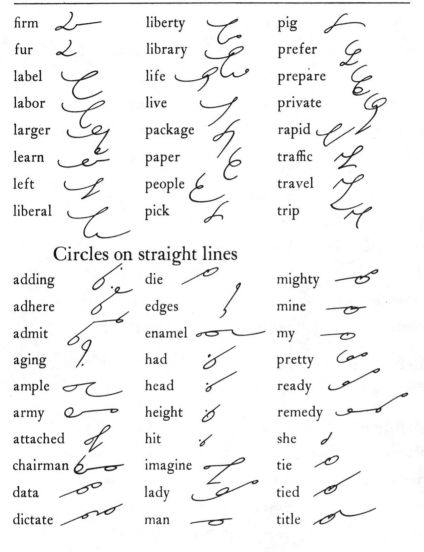

firm	liberty	pig
fur	library	prefer
label	life	prepare
labor	live	private
larger	package	rapid
learn	paper	traffic
left	people	travel
liberal	pick	trip

Circles on straight lines

adding	die	mighty
adhere	edges	mine
admit	enamel	my
aging	had	pretty
ample	head	ready
army	height	remedy
attached	hit	she
chairman	imagine	tie
data	lady	tied
dictate	man	title

Between two reverse curves

| black | car | cargo |
| break | care | carload |

carry	gallon	legal
cracked	gear	paragraph
drag	guilty	rag
fabric	kill	regret
fiber	lack	telegraph
flag	leg	track

O hook on its side

Before *n*

alone	known	stone
drawn	loan	thereon
grown	on	thrown
honor	owner	tone

Before *m*

home	homes	omit

Before *r*

abnormal	floor	narrower
cordial	horn	nor
corn	horses	normal
corner	ignore	or
course	lower	oral
door	moral	orange
drawer	mortgage	organ

origin	storm	tore
original	story	torn
store	torch	

Before *l*

call	golf	recall
coal	hole	roller
collar	holiday	small
college	knowledge	whole
dollar	pay roll	wholesale

Phrases

he calls	on its	on the
I call	on our	on these
on it	on sale	or more

Downward character preceding *o*

ball	fault	salt
baseball	follow	shown
bolt	foreign	solicit
bone	pole	solid
born	policy	solve
borrow	polish	sorrow
borrowers	politics	source
fall	porch	vault

Clockwise *th*

blacksmith	method	theme
death	teeth	thicker
faith	theater	thin

Counterclockwise *th*

Joined to *o*

author	clothing	though
both	growth	thought

Joined to *r*

earth	thorough	three
north	thread	throw

Joined to *l*

lathe	health	healthy

CHAPTER II

LESSON 7

Brief forms

Dear Sir		must		write	
Dear Sirs		right		year	
desire		rights		years	
desires		that		you	
hereto		them		your	
market		to		yours	
Mr.		were		Yours truly	

Phrases

must

he must	I must have	that must be
he must be	I must say	must have
he must have	must be	you must
I must	she must	you must be
I must be	she must be	you must have

that

as that	at that	by that
ask that	before that	for that

21

hope that	that are	that may be
hope that the	that are not	that our
hoping that	that have	that the
if that is	that is	that their
in that	that is not	that there are
is that	that is the	that there is
is that the	that it	that these
of that	that it has	that will
on that	that it is	that will be
on that day	that its	that will not
realize that	that it will	that would
so that	that it will be	that would be
so that the	that may	with that

them

ask them	in them	to them
for them	of them	with them

to

as to	to care	to claim
as to that	to carry	to clean
as to the	to cash	to clear
to call	to catch	to climb
to cancel	to cause	to close

to gain	to its	to their
to get	to taste	to these
to give	to take	to tie
to go	to talk	to trade
to grow	to tell	to train
to his	to that	to travel
to it	to the	to try

you

as you	asking you	if you care
as you are	before you	if you could
as you can	by you	if you get
as you go	can you	if you go
as you have	for you	if you have
as you know	have you	if you have not
as you may	hope you will	if you know
as you may have	give you	if you need
as you say	giving you	if you see
as you will	if you	if you will
as you will see	if you are	if you will be
as you would	if you are not	if you will have
as you would be	if you can	if you will see
ask you	if you can be	if you will ship
asking me	if you cannot	if you would

if you would be	you cannot see	you might
if you would have	you can see	you might be
in which you	you can't	you might have
in which you are	you could	you might not
of you	you could be	you need
reach you	you could have	you need not
serving you	you could not	you say
to have you	you could see	you see
to which you are	you have	you shall have
to you	you have had	you will
which you	you have made	you will be
which you can	you have not	you will have
which you may	you have seen	you will not
with you	you know	you will not be
you are	you made	you will not have
you are not	you make	you will see
you can	you may	you would
you can be	you may be	you would be
you can have	you may have	you would have
you cannot	you may not	you would not

your

as to your	for your	on your
as your	have your	to your
ask your	if your	with your
before your	of your	your name
by your	of yours	your needs

were

if it were	there were	were not

write

I write	I will write	write me

Miscellaneous

for Mr.	I desire	My dear sir
he desires	if you desire	you desire

Word beginning *ex-*

example	expedite	explains
exceed	expense	express
exceeding	expenses	expressed
except	expensive	exterior
excess	expert	extra
excessive	expire	extras
exchange	expires	extreme
exhibit	explain	inexpensive

LESSON 8

Word endings -*tion*, -*tial*, -*cient*, -*ciency*

-*tion*, -*cient*, -*ciency*

action	exemption	portion
ancient	exhibition	possession
application	expansion	precaution
authorization	expiration	preparation
cancellation	expression	prescription
caution	fashion	prevention
collision	illustration	protection
co-operation	mission	ration
collection	motion	relation
corporation	national	section
declaration	occasion	sectional
efficient	operation	selection
efficiency	option	session
election	patient	taxation
exception	physician	vacation

-*tial*

beneficial	financial	partial
essential	initial	social
essentials	official	special

Phrases

for collection ⟋⟍⟍ in relation ⟋⟍⟍

Past tense, *-er, -or*

initialed ⟋	marketed ⟍⟋	writer ⟍
desired ⟍⟋	shipped ⟋⟋	writers ⟍⟍

LESSON 9

Brief forms

been	⟍	pleased	⟍⟋	then	⟍
from	⟍	pleasing	⟍.	they	⟍
like	⟍	should	⟍	was	⟍
please	⟍	than	⟍	when	⟍

Phrases

from

from its ⟍⟋	from his ⟍⟋	from that ⟍⟋
from these ⟍⟋	from it ⟍⟋	from them ⟍⟋
hear from you ⟍⟋	from our ⟍⟋	from you ⟍⟋
from him ⟍⟋	from the ⟍⟋	from which ⟍⟋

like

he liked ⟍⟋	I should not like ⟍⟋	would like ⟍⟋
I like ⟍⟋	if you like ⟍⟋	you liked ⟍⟋
I should like ⟍⟋	if you would like ⟍⟋	you would like ⟍⟋

please

please be	please ship	please write me
please have	please sign	to please
please see	please write	

should

he should	I should have	should not be
he should be	I should say	you should
he should have	should be	you should be
I should	should have	you should have
I should be	should like	you should not

than, then

less than	less than the	since then
less than that	more than	than the

they

as they	that they	they can't
as they are	that they are	they could
before they	that they will	they could not
if they	they are	they have
if they are	they are not	they may
if they are not	they can	they may be
if they can	they can be	they must
if they would	they can have	they will
if they would be	they cannot	they will be

| they will have | they will see | they would buy |
| they will not | they would | they would not |

when

| when our | when the | when they |
| when that | when these | when they are |

was

he was	that it was	was that
I was	that there was	was the
it was	there was	which was
it was the	was it	

Been in phrases

| could have been | have not been | there has been |
| had been | having been | there have been |

Able in phrases

| be able | he will be able | shall be able |
| been able | he will not be able | to be able |

Word endings -*ly*, -*ily*, -*ally*

-*ly*

amply	clearly	earlier
badly	closely	early
barely	daily	excessively
briefly	deeply	extremely

fairly	likely	rapidly
favorably	only	rarely
firmly	mainly	separately
freely	merely	simply
highly	namely	sincerely
inevitably	nearly	slightly
largely	nicely	slowly
lately	possibly	thoroughly

-ily, -ally

cordially	finally	nationally
easily	financially	normally
especially	heartily	occasionally
essentially	heavily	originally
exceptionally	legally	principally
families	locally	readily
family	materially	totally

LESSON 10

The diphthong *oi*

annoyance	boy	coin
annoyed	boys	hoist
avoid	choice	join
boiler	coil	joy

loyal	poison	toy
noise	royal	voice
oil	soil	void

Word endings *-ure, -ture*

failure	lecture	pasture
feature	literature	picture

Word endings *-ual, -tual*

actual	equal	schedules
actually	equally	semiannual

Omission of vowel in word beginnings

re-

reason	region	resale
reasonably	register	research

be-

became	begin	below
because	beginning	behalf
began	begins	betray

de-

debit	deliberate	depot
delays	deposits	derive

des-, dis-

describe	description	despite

destroy   discrepancy   dismissal

disbursed   discretion   dispatch

disclose   disease   display

discouraged   dismiss   dissolved

mis-

miscarry   misleading   mistake

mislaid   misplaced   mistaken

Phrases

he received   I received   to feature

I described   in response   to figure

I disliked   to begin   to join

LESSON 11

Brief forms

after   business   hand

all   businesses   handed

and   businesslike   most

aside   decide   mostly

besides   decided   Mrs.

billing   decidedly   sides

bills   end   what

Phrases

after

after that *(shorthand)*   after them *(shorthand)*   after which *(shorthand)*

after the *(shorthand)*

and

and are *(shorthand)*	and see *(shorthand)*	and they *(shorthand)*
and have *(shorthand)*	and that *(shorthand)*	and was *(shorthand)*
and his *(shorthand)*	and that is *(shorthand)*	and which *(shorthand)*
and is *(shorthand)*	and the *(shorthand)*	and will *(shorthand)*
and our *(shorthand)*	and their *(shorthand)*	and will be *(shorthand)*
and say *(shorthand)*	and these *(shorthand)*	and will not *(shorthand)*

side

he decided *(shorthand)*   I decided *(shorthand)*   if you decide *(shorthand)*

what

what are *(shorthand)*	what is *(shorthand)*	what will *(shorthand)*
what has been *(shorthand)*	what is the *(shorthand)*	what will be *(shorthand)*

Miscellaneous

all right *(shorthand)*   for most *(shorthand)*   of all *(shorthand)*

Any vowel after the diphthong *i*

appliance *(shorthand)*	diameter *(shorthand)*	science *(shorthand)*
bias *(shorthand)*	diet *(shorthand)*	trial *(shorthand)*
diagnosis *(shorthand)*	drier *(shorthand)*	via *(shorthand)*
dial *(shorthand)*	prior *(shorthand)*	violation *(shorthand)*

The dotted circle

appreciate	bacteria	obviate
appreciation	beneficiary	piano
area	create	radiation
areas	depreciation	radiator
association	librarian	variation

Hook and circle vowels joined

drawee	poetry	radio
poems	poets	snowy

LESSON 12

Been in phrases

had not been	I have been	which have been
has been	it has been	would have been
has not been	should have been	you have been
have been	to have been	you have not been

Able in phrases

being able	he should be able	will be able
has been able	he would be able	you may be able
has not been able	I have not been able	you must be able
have been able	I shall be able	you should be able
have not been able	I shall not be able	you will be able
he may be able	I will be able	you would be able

Word beginning *re-*

reappear	refining	reserved
reasons	repair	resources
rebate	repeat	response
receipt	replace	reveal
receive	replied	reverse
reception	reservation	revise
rechecked	reserve	revision

E written in *re-*

reclaim	regain	rename
recline	remake	retake

Word beginning *de-*

decision	deposit	deserve
delay	depositor	design
delayed	depository	designer

E written in *de-*

decay	declare	decline

CHAPTER III

LESSON 13

The *oo* hook

ŭ

above	drug	shovels
apparatus	duck	status
blood	dug	stub
bud	dust	stuff
bulbs	illustrate	suction
bulk	illustrations	suffer
butter	luck	sufficient
chorus	oven	thus
color	plug	tough
couple	plus	truck
cup	production	trust
cups	reduction	tub
cut	reproduction	uneven
disastrous	rough	up
discussion	rub	upper
does	rubber	utterly

ŏŏ

book	foot	looked
booked	full	pull
bushel	fully	push
cook	hook	stood
cooker	look	sugar
		took

ōō

accrued	grew	route
blue	group	routine
booth	grouped	rule
boots	jewel	school
bouquet	jewelers	screw
cool	jewelry	shoe
coupon	juvenile	spoon
crude	loose	through
do	lose	tool
drew	pool	tooth
exclude	poor	tour
exclusive	prune	true
food	roof	who
fruit	room	whom
glued	root	withdrew

Phrases

do, does

do it	if you do	you do not like
do not	if you do not	does not
do not have	if you do not like	does not have
do so	that do not	he does
do you	they do	he does not
I do	they do not	that does not
I do not	you do	this does not
I do not like	you do not	which does

who, whom

who are	who knows	who should
who can	who like	who should be
who can be	who made	who takes
who cannot	who make	who taught
who could	who makes	who will
who desire	who may	who will be
who do not	who may be	who would
who go	who might	who would be
who have	who might be	who would have
who have had	who might have.	who would like
who have made	who might like	who would not
who is	who must	to whom

Miscellaneous

above the	I took	to choose
check up	I trust	to cut
for whom	through its	to fuss
he discussed	through that	to push
he looks	through the	to shoot
he took	through them	to trust
I discussed	through these	up to
I look	to book	up to the

Words beginning w, sw, wh

wa

highway	waiver	wear
wages	waste	wears
wagon	wave	weigh
waist	way	weighed
wait	ways	weight

wi

wide	wire	wise
wife	wires	wives

we

we	width	worries
west	win	worse
wet	witness	worst

wo

walk	warm	water
wall	wash	woe
walnut	washer	worn
war	watch	woven

woo

wool	woolen	wood

sw

swam	sweet	swivel
swear	swell	sworn
sweater	switch	swollen

wh

whale	wheel	whip
wheat	while	white

Phrases

as we	if we do	we can have
as we are	if we have	we can make
as we have	we are	we cannot
if we	we are not	we cannot be
if we can	we are sure	we can say
if we can be	we call	we can't
if we cannot	we can	we could
if we could	we can be	we could be

we could have	we have not had	we shall not
we could not	we know	we shall not be able
we decide	we made	we shall see
we decided	we make	we should
we desire	we may	we should be
we do	we may be	we should have
we do not	we may be able	we should like
we do not say	we may have	we should not like
we do not see	we mean	we should say
we feel	we might	we take
we feel sure	we might be able	we took
we get	we must	we tried
we give	we must have	we trust
we have	we need	we try
we have been	we note	we will
we have been able	we notice	we will be
we have decided	we shall	we will have
we have given	we shall be	we will not
we have had	we shall be able	we will not be
we have made	we shall have	we will see
we have not	we shall mail	we will ship
we have not been	we shall make	we would
we have not been able	we shall need	we would be

we would have	⟋⟋	we would not	⟋	which we	⟋
we would like	⟋⟍	we would not be able	⟋	which we are	⟋

LESSON 14

Brief forms

about		gladly		thing	
booklet		let		think	
enclose		letter		this	
enclosed		letters		very	
enclosure		nothing		worth	
glad		send		worthy	

Phrases

about

about it		about that		about these	
about its		about the		about this	
about my		about them		about which	
				about your	

this

after this		do this		if this is	
as this		for this		if this is not	
at this		from this		if this is the	
before this		hope that this		in this	
by this		if this		in this case	

in this way   this is   this was the

of this   this is not   this will

on this   this is the   this would

on this side   this man   this would be

since this   this may   to this

that this   this may be   up to this

that this is   this means   when this

this can be   this was   with this

let, letter

and let   I have your letter   please let

as your letter   if you let   this letter

do not let   in that letter   we have your letter

for your letter   let me   your letter

thing, think

as you think   I think   to think

if you think   if they think   we do not think

do you think   same thing   who think

I do not think   they think   you think

glad

be glad   I shall be glad   we shall be glad

he will be glad   I should be glad   we would be glad

he would be glad   shall be glad   will be glad

I am glad   they will be glad

send

please send   send this   sending the

send him   send us   sending them

send them   send you   sending us

sending you

very

very glad   very good   very well

enclose

I enclose   we enclose   you enclosed

Word ending *-ther*

another	father	mother
bother	feather	neither
bothered	gather	rather
brother	other	together
either	others	weather
farther	leather	whether

Phrases

each other	other side	to gather
he gathered	other than	whether or not
I gathered	to bother	

LESSON 15

The sound of *w* in the body of a word

Broadway	quick	roadway
dwelling	quicker	railway
equip	quiet	requisition
equipped	quit	reservoir
liquid	quite	square
queen	quota	twice
query	quote	twin

Phrases

to quit	to quote	we quoted

Ah, aw

ahead	awaiting	aware
await	awake	away

The sound of *y*

yacht	yeast	yes
yarn	yell	yoke
yarns	yellow	youth

LESSON 16

Brief forms

belief	believer	delivered
believe	deliver	deliveries

doctor	return	satisfied
during	returned	satisfy
necessarily	satisfaction	work
necessary	satisfactorily	worked
next	satisfactory	yet

Phrases

as necessary	I believe	next meeting
as yet	I do not believe	next year
has not yet	I returned	next year's
has not yet been	if necessary	of work
have not yet	in return	please return
he returns	is not yet	to believe

Omission of short ŭ

Before *n*

begun	lunch	runs
bunch	luncheon	son
done	punch	sun
gun	run	ton
fun	runner	tonnage

Before *m*

become	column	drum
bumper	come	lumber

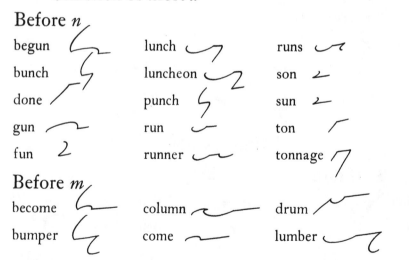

lump   ⟍⟋   some   ⟋   summary ⟋⟋

plumbing ⊂⟋   something ⟋⟋·   summer ⟋⟋

pump   ⟋⟋   sum   ⟋   welcome ⟋⟋

Before a downstroke

brush   ⟋   crushed ⟋⟋   rush   ⟋

brushed ⟋   flush   ⟋⟋   rushed ⟋

budget   ⟋   judge   ⟋   rushing ⟋.

clutch   ⟋   much ⟋⟋   touch   ⟋

Phrases

as much   ⟋   I have done   ⟋   to be done   ⟋

be done   ⟋   I come   ⟋   to become   ⟋

being done ⟋   much more ⟋   to come   ⟋

can be done ⟋   much more than   to judge   ⟋

cannot be done ⟋   must be done ⟋   too much ⟋

can't be done ⟋   please rush ⟋   very much ⟋

could be done ⟋   should be done ⟋ we have done ⟋

has come   ⟋   so much   ⟋   who comes ⟋

has done   ⟋   something like ⟋ who have done ⟋

have done   ⟋   they come ⟋   will be done   ⟋

                                         would be done   ⟋

Strokes for *ng* and *ngk*

ng

angle	ring	string
bring	shingle	strong
hanger	sing	strongly
hung	single	swing
king	song	tongue
language	spring	wrong
length	strength	young

ngk

anchor	crank	link
ankle	drinking	pink
bank	frank	sanction
banker	frankly	shrinkage
bankruptcy	functions	sink
banquet	handkerchief	tank
blank	ink	trunk
blanket	junction	uncle

LESSON 17

Brief forms

accompanied	among	bookkeeping
along	belong	companies

company	over	thank
great	overcharge	under
greater	overlooked	undercharges
greatly	oversight	undersized
keep	oversize	understood
kept	remit	where
long	remittance	whereabouts
longer	remittances	whereas
nowhere	remitted	wherein

Phrases

along the	thank you for this
along this	thank you for your
among the	thank you for your letter
among them	this company
among these	to keep
as long	to thank you for
if you keep	to thank you for your
so long	we thank you for
thank you	we thank you for the
thank you for	we thank you for your
thank you for the	

Strokes for *rd* and *ld*

rd

accordance	favored	preferred
answered	garden	prepared
appeared	guard	record
assured	harder	registered
award	hard	repaired
awarded	hardly	retired
bird	hardware	seaboard
board	hazard	stored
border	heard	suffered
burden	hired	third
card	ignored	tired
colored	occurred	toward
cord	offered	word
corduroy	orchard	wired
expired	pardon	yard

ld

billed	canceled	failed
boiled	child	field
build	children	filed
builders	cold	filled
called	drilled	fold

folded	holders	sealed
folder	holds	settled
gold	mailed	shoulder
golden	milled	soiled
handled	old	sold
hauled	older	spoiled
held	pulled	told
hold	rolled	yield

Phrases

rd

good natured   to board   to burden

ld

I called	he sold	to build
I told	he told	we failed
I traveled	old-fashioned	we filled
has called	so-called	we mailed
he called	to behold	

LESSON 18

OO hook on its side

annum	move	noon
bonus	mud	nut
enormous	muslin	remove
famous	none	smooth

Word endings *-ure, -ual*

-ure

fixtures	natural	secure
mature	naturally	signature
moisture	pictures	structure
nature	procure	structural

-ual

annual	gradual	scheduling
annually	gradually	virtually

After a downstroke

assurance	measure	surely
assure	measures	treasurer
assures	pleasure	treasury
juries	pressure	casually
jury	sure	visual

Phrases

sure

be sure	feeling sure	to be sure
being sure	I am sure	you can be sure
can be sure	if you are sure	you may be sure
feel sure	please be sure	

The combination *us*

adjust	choose	justly
adjusts	desirous	nervous
ambitious	discuss	religious
anxious	discussed	shoes
anxiously	just	us
bus	justice	whose

Phrases

before us	gave us	on us
by us	give us	to give us
for us	giving us	with us
from us	hear from us	

Comma *s* with *f, v, k, g*; left *s* with *p, b, r, l*

accept	busy	decrease
address	basket	drastic
answer	cancel	elastic
apiece	capacity	errors
applies	case	facilitate
arisen	cast	fails
arrives	checks	fast
ask	cigars	favors
backs	class	feels
bags	clerks	fiscal

gas	pencil	service
gasoline	piece	shelves
girls	pigs	sketch
gives	pipes	space
glass	raise	specific
graphs	realize	speed
grocery	release	separate
guess	risk	spirit
helps	ropes	spoke
lamps	sacrifice	spread
lease	safety	supplied
least	salary	surprise
less	sales	tags
list	salesman	teachers
listen	scheme	tracer
lives	score	trips
makes	scrap	vast
maps	search	vicinity
marks	secretary	visit
parcel	sells	wholesale
pass	series	

Comma *s* before *t, d, n, m, o;* left *s* after those characters

absence	fellows	miss
advance	finance	names
agencies	firms	needs
arms	frames	notice
astray	frozen	pins
assets	glance	plans
balance	grades	post
bids	gross	practice
chance	happens	principal
chosen	hats	rates
Christmas	heads	rose
city	homes	sad
claims	illness	said
close	knows	sample
coast	ladies	seats
courtesy	lessons	sedan
currency	lines	seems
days	machines	semester
desk	magazine	sense
establishing	means	set
farms	medicine	shades

sheets	smoke	statistics
shows	snap	step
sickness	soap	still
sign	solicit	story
similar	source	style
simple	staff	task
since	stamp	tickets
sincere	start	vacancies

Comma *s* before and after *sh, ch, j*

branches	dishes	packages
bridges	ditches	pages
changes	edges	reaches
charges	hinges	sash
cheese	matches	siege
chest	messages	wrenches

Words consisting of *s* or *s* and *th* and a circle vowel

as	say	seethe
has	see	these

CHAPTER IV

LESSON 19

The diphthong *u*

acute	fewer	tube
argue	fuel	unique
bureau	peculiar	unite
cubic	pure	unit
cure	review	utilization
dispute	reviews	view
few	tribune	views

The diphthong *ow*

aloud	flowers	power
blouse	loud	proud
bow	mouth	south
cow	now	southeast
crowd	ounce	towels
doubt	plow	tower
flour	powder	voucher

Phrases

in view	I doubt	right now
few days	in our power	we doubt

Brief forms

ever		one		use	
every		out		used	
how		outline		whatever	
importance		outside		whenever	
important		soon		wherever	
matters		sooner		without	
once		those		won	

Phrases

about those		for one		one-half	
along those		for one thing		one way	
among those		for those		one year	
and those		from those		only one	
as those		how much		that those	
at those		in this matter		this matter	
by those		in those		this one	
each one		of those		to those	
ever since		one thing		very important	
every one		on this matter		when those	
every other		once more		with those	

LESSON 20

Brief forms

always ⌒	suggest	weak ⌒
any	suggested	week ⌒
anyone	suggestion	weekly
anything	unable	wish
gone	unusually	wished
several	usual	world

Phrases

always be	for any one	if anything
any more	for any other	if you wish
any one	for anything	of any
any other	has gone	one week
any others	have gone	several days
business world	I wish	several other
for any	if any	several others

Blended consonants *ted, ded, det*

ted

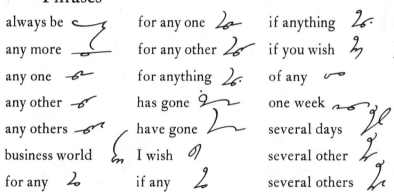

accepted	adopted	benefited
adapted	appreciated	co-operated
adjusted	asserted	created
admitted	awaited	delighted

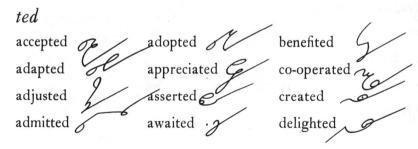

depleted	listed	solicited
deposited	noted	started
doubted	omitted	steadily
executed	operated	steady
excited	pasted	studied
exhibited	posted	studies
fitted	quoted	study
hesitated	rated	today
homestead	related	treated
illustrated	repeated	united
lifted	repeatedly	visited
limited	routed	waited
liquidated	separated	wasted

ded

added	deductions	headed
dead	graded	loaded
deduction	guided	needed

det, dit

audit	credits	detailed
auditor	debt	ditto
credit	debtor	editor
credited	detail	editorial

Phrases

he needed   I needed   I noted

Blended consonants *m-n, m-m*

administer	manner	minimum
aluminum	manual	minute
cement	many	money
eliminate	maximum	month
examine	meant	monthly
examiner	member	nominal
examined	memo	prominence
freshmen	memorial	remain
harmony	memory	remained
human	men	romance
immensely	mental	salesmen
lemon	mention	summons
manage	mentioned	tremendous
manager	mineral	woman
managers	miniature	women

Phrases

as many	few minutes	I doubted
each month	few months	I mention
every minute	he mentioned	I mentioned
every month	how many	I remain

in this manner	next month	this month
in this month's	several months	to mention
many other	so many	we mention
many others	these men	you mentioned

LESSON 21

Blended consonants *nt, nd*

nt

absent	current	parents
acquainted	disappoint	plant
apparent	eccentric	planted
applicant	event	pleasant
appointed	eventually	plenty
aunt	excellent	point
bent	front	prevent
brilliant	grant	prevented
cent	granted	printer
center	guarantee	prominent
central	hints	recent
centralized	hunting	rent
century	joint	rental
client	jointly	rented
country	paint	sent

silent	venture	went
talent	warrant	winter
vacant	warranted	won't

nd

assigned	designed	outlined
band	fastened	owned
behind	find	phoned
beyond	friend	planned
bind	fund	refund
binder	gained	render
bindery	grand	rendered
blunder	grind	sand
bond	island	sandals
bonded	joined	second
brand	kind	secondary
burned	kindness	signed
calendar	land	splendid
candy	lands	surrender
canned	learned	surrendered
cleaned	lend	trained
cylinder	lined	trend
earned	loaned	unearned
explained	overburdened	wind

Phrases

aren't	I sent	we don't
as you will find	if we don't	we find
doesn't	if you don't	we shouldn't
don't	isn't	we wouldn't
hadn't	isn't it	weren't
hasn't	shouldn't	who doesn't
haven't	they don't	who isn't
he couldn't	to bind	will find
he finds	to find	wouldn't
he isn't	to paint	you aren't
I couldn't	to plant	you couldn't
I don't	to point	you don't
I find	to prevent	you haven't
I haven't	to print	you will find
I learned	we couldn't	you wouldn't

Blended consonants *mt, md*

ashamed	framed	prompt
claimed	fumed	promptly
deemed	gummed	promptness
exempt	jammed	seemed
famed	named	trimmed

Initial vowel omitted

anticipate	endorse	entry
anticipated	endorsed	index
anticipation	endorser	indexes
antique	entire	industry
emptied	entirely	intelligence
empty	entitled	into

Phrases

| into it | into the | into these |
| into that | into them | into this |

Brief forms

big	did	office
bigger	general	offices
bigness	generally	officers
date	got	opportunity
dated	individual	want
dates	morning	wanted

Phrases

as you did	he didn't	I got
did not	he got	if you did not
didn't	I did	if you didn't
he did	I did not	next morning
he did not	I didn't	office manager

on that date	we did	who didn't
they did	we did not	you did
this date	we didn't	you did not
this morning	we got	you didn't

LESSON 22

Omission of vowels
Circle omitted from *u*

absolute	manufacture	produced
avenue	manufactured	producers
due	manufacturer	produces
dues	manuscript	reduce
duly	music	reduced
duty	mutual	reduces
enumerated	mutually	renew
induce	new	renewal
issue	newer	renewed
issued	news	revenue
issues	numerous	suit
knew	overdue	suited
lieu	produce	volume

Other vowel omissions

auditorium	millions	serious
courteous	miscellaneous	seriously
erroneous	period	situated
genuine	premium	theory
graduate	previous	union
graduation	previously	vacuum
ideal	radius	various

Phrases

he knew	in lieu	we knew
I knew	to produce	you knew

Days and months

Sunday	January	July
Monday	February	August
Tuesday	March	September
Wednesday	April	October
Thursday	May	November
Friday	June	December
Saturday		

Phrases

Friday morning	Tuesday morning
Friday night	Wednesday morning
Saturday morning	Thursday morning

LESSON 23

Omission of *ow*

around	count	down
account	counted	found
accountant	counter	foundry
accounted	counting	ground
background	county	round
brown	crown	sound
council	discount	surrounding
counsel	discounted	town

moun

amount	amounting	mount
amounted	amounts	mounted

jog

announce	announced	announces

Phrases

he found	to count	we found
I found	we count	

Word beginnings *per-*, *pro-*, *pur-*

per-

per	percentage	perhaps
per cent	perforated	permanent

permit ⌒   person   personnel

permitted   personal   persuade

perpetual   personally   persuaded

perplexing   persons   persuasion

pro-

approach   proceed   proof

approached   process   proper

appropriate   processes   properly

appropriation   professional   proportion

approval   professor   proportionate

approve   profit   proprietor

approved   profitably   prosperous

approximate   prohibit   prove

apron   promise   proved

fireproofing   promised   proven

probate   promises   provide

problem   promote   provided

procedure   promotion   provision

pur-

purloin   pursuant   pursued

purple   pursue   pursuit

Phrases

it will prove	to permit	to promote
per hour	to persuade	to prove
per month	to proceed	to provide

-ment

adjustment	endorsement	monument
agreement	equipment	movement
allotment	establishment	nonpayment
announcement	experiment	ornamental
appointment	experimental	payment
arrangement	fundamental	replacement
assessment	garment	settlement
assignment	inducement	shipment
basement	judgment	supplement
casement	management	supplemental
document	measurement	supplementary
elementary	moment	treatment
elements	momentary	

Phrases

few moments	in payment

-ble

acceptable	adjustable	agreeable
adaptable	advisable	applicable

appreciable	favorable	reasonable
available	feasible	reliable
cable	flexible	responsible
capable	inadvisable	salable
desirable	liable	suitable
double	payable	table
eligible	possible	trouble
equitable	profitable	unaccountable

CHAPTER V

LESSON 25

-ship

fellowship	membership	scholarship
hardship	ownership	steamship
kinship	relationship	township

-cle, -cal

analytical	mechanical	practical
article	mechanically	practically
chemical	medical	radical
chemicals	musical	statistical
critical	periodical	surgical
geographical	periodically	technical
historical	physical	typical
logical	political	typographical

-self, -selves

herself	myself	themselves
himself	oneself	yourself
itself	ourselves	yourselves

Phrases

for itself	for themselves	in itself
for myself	for yourself	of ourselves
for ourselves	for yourselves	with themselves

After-

aftermath	afternoon	afterthought

LESSON 26

Brief forms

enable	progressive	speaks
order	property	street
ordered	purpose	streets
orders	purposes	such
progress	speak	upon

Phrases

in order	on such	upon this
in order that	to speak	upon us
in such	upon such	upon which
no such	upon the	upon you
of such	upon them	with such

Blended consonants *pent, pend, gent*

pent, pend

appendix	carpenter	depend

dependable   expended   respondent

depended   expenditure   spend

dependent   happened   spent

depends   opened   suspend

expend   pending

gent

cogent   gentle   intelligently

diligently   gentleman   urgent

genteel   intelligent   urgently

Blended consonants *def, dev, tive*

def

defense   devised   difference

defer   develop   different

deferred   developed   diversion

defiance   development   divert

definite   develops   diverted

defy   devote   divide

device   devoted   divided

devise   differ   division

tive

appreciative   co-operative   descriptive

authoritative   creative   executive

initiative   native   positively

locomotive   negative   relative

motive   positive   scientific

Phrases

to spend   to defeat   to devote

LESSON 27

Electr-, electric

electric   electrician   electronics

electrical   electricity   electros

electrically   electric wire   electrotype

Inter-

interfere   intermediate   interrupted

interference   internal   interruption

interim   international   interval

interior   interpreted   interview

intr-

introduce   introduced   introduction

enter-

enter   entering   entrance

entered   enterprise   entrances

Short-

short	/	shortages	//	shorter	'‿
shortage	//	shorten	/_	shortly	'6

ship-

shipwreck	'‿o	shipshape	/6	shipmate	'—6

LESSON 28

Words modified in phrases

as soon as

as soon as 2ᴜ   as soon as possible 2ᴜ   as soon as the 2ᴜ

hope

I hope	I hope to see	we hope these
I hope that	we hope	we hope this
I hope that the	we hope that	we hope to have
I hope the	we hope that these	we hope you can
I hope these	we hope that this	we hope you will
I hope this	we hope the	

I had

I had	I had been	I had not

us

let us	let us know	please let us
let us have	let us say	to us

to

to do	to do the	to himself
to do it	to do this	to our
to do so	to him	to ourselves

order

if your order	thank you for your order	your order
of your order	you ordered	your orders

Miscellaneous

of course	of course it is	worth while

Use of blend for *not*

he wasn't	it is not	that it was not
I was not	it isn't	there isn't
if it isn't	it was not	this was not
if it was not	it wasn't	was not
if there is not	that it is not	wasn't

Ago in phrases

centuries ago	months ago	some years ago
few days ago	several days ago	weeks ago
few months ago	several months ago	years ago
long ago	some weeks ago	

Want in phrases

he wanted	I want	if you want
he wants	I wanted	they want

we want		who want		you want	
we wanted		who wanted		you wanted	

LESSON 29

Word endings -*ful*, -*ify*

-*ful*

awful		doubtful		hopeful	
beautiful		faithful		powerful	
careful		grateful		thoughtful	
carefully		helpful		useful	
delightful		helpfulness		usefulness	

-*ify*

amplifier		diversified		notify	
amplify		gratified		ratify	
beautify		gratifying		specified	
certified		justified		specify	
certify		justify		testify	
classified		modify		verify	

Phrases

to beautify		to specify		to verify	

-*ification*

classification		modification		ratification	
edification		notification		specifications	
justification		qualifications		verification	

-gram

| cablegram | monogram | telegram |
| diagram | program | telegrams |

-rity

authorities	majority	securities
charity	maturity	security
clarity	prosperity	surety

-lity

ability	inability	possibilities
advisability	liabilities	qualities
disability	locality	reliability
facilities	nobility	responsibility
facility	personality	sensibilities

-lty

| casualty | loyalty | royalty |
| faculty | penalty | |

CHAPTER VI

LESSON 31

Blended consonants *ten, den*

ten

acceptance	extensively	stenographer
attend	extent	stenographic
attended	gotten	straighten
attention	hesitancy	straightened
bulletin	itinerary	tenant
button	maintenance	tend
carton	patent	tender
cotton	retention	tendered
destined	rotten	tent
distance	satin	tentative
extension	sentence	tonight
extensive	standard	written

den

abandon	audience	dinner
accident	danger	evidence
attendance	deny	evident

80

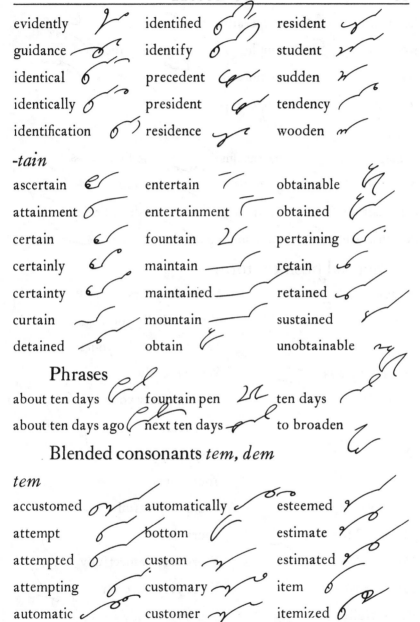

evidently   identified   resident

guidance   identify   student

identical   precedent   sudden

identically   president   tendency

identification   residence   wooden

-tain

ascertain   entertain   obtainable

attainment   entertainment   obtained

certain   fountain   pertaining

certainly   maintain   retain

certainty   maintained   retained

curtain   mountain   sustained

detained   obtain   unobtainable

Phrases

about ten days   fountain pen   ten days

about ten days ago   next ten days   to broaden

Blended consonants tem, dem

tem

accustomed   automatically   esteemed

attempt   bottom   estimate

attempted   custom   estimated

attempting   customary   item

automatic   customer   itemized

legitimate	temperature	timber
stomach	temple	tomatoes
system	temporarily	tomorrow
temper	temporary	

dem

damage	dimensions	medium
damaged	domestic	random
demonstrate	freedom	redemption
demonstration	kingdom	seldom

Special business forms

to know		Sincerely yours
to make		Very cordially yours
to me		Very respectfully yours
Cordially yours		Very sincerely
Dear Madam		Very sincerely yours
Dear Miss		Very truly
Dear Mrs.		Very truly yours
Dear Mr.		Yours cordially
Gentlemen		Yours respectfully
My dear Miss		Yours sincerely
My dear Mr.		Yours very respectfully
My dear Mrs.		Yours very sincerely
Respectfully yours		Yours very truly

LESSON 32

Brief forms

difficult	outstanding	standing
difficulty	purchase	standpoint
extraordinary	purchased	stands
meantime	purchases	time
merchandise	purchasing	times
merchant	sometime	understand
ordinarily	sometimes	understandable
ordinary	stand	why

Phrases

about that time	by the time	on time
about the time	by this time	one time
about this time	each time	several times
after that time	few times	since that time
any time	for the time	some time
at all times	from time	some time ago
at that time	in time	such time
at the time	long time	that time
at this time	many times	this time
at which time	next time	to purchase
before that time	of that time	to time
by that time	of time	why not

Tern, term; dern, derm; thern, therm

attorney	modern	termed
determine	northern	terminal
determined	northwestern	terminate
eastern	pattern	terms
eternal	southeastern	thermometer
external	southern	turn
fraternity	southwestern	turned
lantern	term	western

Phrases

| he turned | I turned | to turn |

Syllable *ort*

assorted	port	report
assortment	portable	reported
court	portfolio	reports
deportment	ports	resort
export	quart	sort
headquarters	quarter	sport
mortal	quarterly	sports

LESSON 33

-ct

abstract	effect	productive
act	effective	project
acted	elect	prospect
active	exact	prospective
actively	exactly	protect
activity	expect	protected
acts	expected	reflect
affect	expects	reflected
affected	fact	rejected
affects	facts	respect
attractive	inactive	respectfully
collect	intact	respectively
collected	neglected	select
deduct	perfect	selected
deducted	perfectly	strictly
defect	predict	tract
district	product	tractor

Phrases

affect the	fact that this	to perfect
fact that	in fact	to protect
fact that the	to collect	to select

One-syllable words ending in *st*

best		last		rested	
cost		lasting		resting	
costing		lasts		rests	
costly		past		test	
costs		past-due		tested	
first		rest		tests	

Phrases

at last		in the last		last time	
first time		last minute		last year	
for the last		last month		last year's	
for the past		last night		past year	

-*st*

against		earnestly		honestly	
artist		exhaust		honesty	
assist		exhausted		interest	
assistance		exist		interested	
assistant		existed		interesting	
attested		existence		interests	
cheapest		exists		kindest	
chemistry		finest		largest	
closest		harvest		latest	
earnest		honest		nearest	

protest *(outline)*   quickest *(outline)*   resistance *(outline)*

protested *(outline)*   resist *(outline)*   slightest *(outline)*

Phrases

against the *(outline)*   to protest *(outline)*   against your *(outline)*

Disjoined word endings -*ist*, -*est*

earliest *(outline)*   highest *(outline)*   prettiest *(outline)*

easiest *(outline)*   lowest *(outline)*   shortest *(outline)*

greatest *(outline)*   newest *(outline)*   slowest *(outline)*

LESSON 34

Brief forms

advertise *(outline)*   else *(outline)*   presented *(outline)*

advertisement *(outline)*   elsewhere *(outline)*   probable *(outline)*

body *(outline)*   part *(outline)*   probably *(outline)*

consider *(outline)*   participate *(outline)*   remember *(outline)*

considerably *(outline)*   parties *(outline)*   represent *(outline)*

consideration *(outline)*   party *(outline)*   representative *(outline)*

considered *(outline)*   presence *(outline)*   represented *(outline)*

departing *(outline)*   present *(outline)*   represents *(outline)*

Phrases

anyone else *(outline)*   he considers *(outline)*   into consideration *(outline)*

anything else *(outline)*   I consider *(outline)*   nothing else *(outline)*

at present *(outline)*   I remember *(outline)*   on our part *(outline)*

he considered *(outline)*   if you consider *(outline)*

remember that	to part	we shall consider
something else	to present	which we consider
to consider	we consider	you will remember

Omission of *d*

amend	diamond	pound
amended	dividend	pounds
amendment	extend	recommend
bound	extended	recommended
bundles	extends	remind
demand	mind	reminded

LESSON 35

Incl-

inclement	include	included
inclined	includes	inclusive

Post-

postage	posthaste	postpaid
postal	postmark	postpone
post card	postmaster	postponed
postdate	post office	postscript

Super-, supr-

superb	supervision	supports
superficially	supervisor	supremacy
superior	support	supreme

Trans-

transact	transit	transmittal
transaction	transition	transmitted
transfer	translated	transparent
transferred	translation	transcribe
transfers	transmit	transcript

CHAPTER VII

LESSON 37

Con-

concealed	confess	consign
concentrate	confidential	consigned
conception	confine	consignee
concern	confined	consignment
concerned	confirm	consist
concerns	confirmed	consisted
concert	conflict	consistent
concession	congested	consistently
concrete	congestion	consists
condense	conjunction	consolidate
condensed	connected	constant
conduct	connection	constantly
conducted	connections	construct
conductor	conscientious	constructed
confer	consent	construction
conference	conservative	constructive

90

contact

contain

contained

container

contemplate

contemplated

content

contention

contest

continent

contingent

continuance

continue

continued

continues

continuous

contract

contracted

contractor

contracts

contrary

contrast

control

controversy

convention

conversation

conversion

convert

converted

convey

convince

discontinue

discontinued

reconcile

reconstruction

com-

accommodate

accomplish

accomplished

combine

command

commence

commend

comment

commerce

commercial

commitments

committed

committee

commodities

commodity

common

commonly

communities

community

compact

companion

comparative

compare

compared

comparison

compel

compelled

compensation

compete

competent

competitive

completed

comply

competitor

completely

compound

competitors

completion

comprehensive

compiled

compliance

compressor

complaint

compliment

comedian

complete

complimentary

comedies

Phrases

to compare

to conceal

to consist

to complain

to confide

to continue

to complete

to confirm

to convince

to comply

to conserve

we continue

En-

encountered

engaged

enjoy

encourage

engagement

enjoyed

encouraged

engine

enlarge

encouragement

engineer

enrolled

encroachment

engineers

en route

endeavor

engrave

enthusiastic

engage

engraver

enthusiasm

in-

incapable

incident

income

incentive

incidental

incorporated

inch

incidentally

increase

increased	inside	intend
increases	insist	intended
incurred	insisted	intends
indebted	inspection	intention
indebtedness	inspiration	intimate
indeed	install	intimated
indemnity	installation	invariably
infants	installed	inventory
infer	installment	invest
inferior	instead	invested
inferred	instruct	investment
influence	instructed	invite
injured	instruction	invited
injuries	instructor	invoice
injury	instructive	invoiced
inlaid	instrument	invoices
insert	insurance	involved
inserted	insure	superintendent
insertion	insured	

un-

uncertain	undoubtedly	unfilled
unclaimed	unduly	unjust
undecided	unfair	unloaded

| unpacked | unreasonable | unsettled |
| unpaid | unsatisfactory | until |

unn-

| unknown | unnecessary | unnoticed |

Phrases

| we invite | you intend | who intend |
| we insist | we intend | your intention |

Em-

embarrass	emphasis	employed
embarrassment	emphatically	employees
embraces	empire	employment

im-

impairment	impossible	imprinting
impartial	impracticable	improper
imperative	impress	improved
implements	impressed	improvement
import	impression	reimburse
imported	imprint	reimbursed
imports	imprinted	reimbursement

imm-

| immodest | immoral | immortal |

LESSON 38

For-, fore-

afford ⟋

effort ⟋

efforts ⟋

force ⟋

forced ⟋

foreclosure ⟋

foreman ⟋

forerunner ⟋

forget ⟋

form ⟋

formal ⟋

former ⟋

formerly ⟋

forms ⟋

forth ⟋

fortune ⟋

fourth ⟋

inform ⟋

informed ⟋

misfortune ⟋

unfortunate ⟋

fur-

furlough ⟋

furnace ⟋

furnaces ⟋

furnish ⟋

furnished ⟋

furnishing ⟋

furniture ⟋

further ⟋

furthermore ⟋

Phrases

inform us ⟋

inform you ⟋

informing us ⟋

set forth ⟋

setting forth ⟋

to force ⟋

to forego ⟋

to forget ⟋

to forfeit ⟋

to form ⟋

to furnish ⟋

to perform ⟋

Al-

almost ⟋

already ⟋

also ⟋

alter ⟋

alterations ⟋

alternate ⟋

alternatives ⟋

although ⟋

altogether ⟋

Sub-

subchief	submit	subscription
subdivision	submitted	substance
subeditor	subordinate	substantial
subhead	subscribe	substantiate
sublet	subscriber	subtracted
		subway

Ul-

adult	culminate	resulted
agriculture	culture	resulting
consult	multiple	results
consulted	result	ultimate

-ward

afterward	backward	onward
awkward	forward	reward
awkwardly	forwarded	upward

-hood

boyhood	hardihood	neighborhood
childhood	manhood	parenthood

Phrases

I submit	to consult	to forward

LESSON 39

Abbreviating principle

-use

accuse · confusing · inexcusable

accusation · confusion · refusal

confuse · excuse · refused

confused · excuses · refuses

-titude

aptitude · fortitude · latitude

attitude · gratitude · multitude

-cate

adequate · duplicate · indicates

advocate · duplicated · locate

certificate · inadequate · located

communicate · indicate · reciprocate

confiscate · indicated · syndicate

-cation

allocation · duplication · eradication

communication · education · indication

confiscation · educational · location

-gate

aggregate · corrugated · investigate

-gation

investigation ⟋ irrigation ⟋ obligation ⟍

Phrases ⟋

I refuse ⟋ to confuse ⟋

LESSON 40

Abbreviating principle (continued)

-quire

acquire	inquire	require
acquirement	inquiries	required
esquire	inquiry	requirements

-ntic

Atlantic	authentic	frantic

-ology

apology	biology	psychological
apologies	physiology	technology
apologize	psychology	terminology

-tribute

attribute	contribution	distribution
contribute	distribute	distributors
contributed	distributed	retribution

-quent

consequently	eloquent	frequently
delinquent	frequent	subsequent

-itis

appendicitis   *shorthand*   tonsillitis   *shorthand*   neuritis   *shorthand*

-iety

variety   *shorthand*   society   *shorthand*   propriety   *shorthand*

-titute, -titution

constitute   *shorthand*   institution   *shorthand*   substitute   *shorthand*

institute   *shorthand*   restitution   *shorthand*   substitution   *shorthand*

LESSON 41

Abbreviating principle (concluded)

algebra   *shorthand*   curriculum   *shorthand*   memorandums   *shorthand*

alphabet   *shorthand*   inconvenience   *shorthand*   philosophy   *shorthand*

alphabetical   *shorthand*   inconvenienced   *shorthand*   preliminary   *shorthand*

arithmetic   *shorthand*   inconvenient   *shorthand*   privilege   *shorthand*

convenience   *shorthand*   equivalent   *shorthand*   privileges   *shorthand*

convenient   *shorthand*   memoranda   *shorthand*   privileged   *shorthand*

conveniently   *shorthand*   memorandum   *shorthand*   reluctant   *shorthand*

-tition, -tation, -dition, -dation, -nition, -nation,
-mition, -mation

accommodation   *shorthand*   combination   *shorthand*   competition   *shorthand*

addition   *shorthand*   commendation   *shorthand*   condition   *shorthand*

additional   *shorthand*   commission   *shorthand*   confirmation   *shorthand*

admission   *shorthand*   commissioner   *shorthand*   consolidation   *shorthand*

consultation	imitation	recommendation
destination	information	repetition
discrimination	interpretation	reputation
donation	invitation	solicitation
edition	notation	station
estimation	omission	stationed
examination	permission	stationery
explanation	petition	suspension
foundation	quotation	transmission
hesitation	recitation	transportation

Phrases

any information   in addition   to petition

CHAPTER VIII

LESSON 43

Words omitted in phrases

able to work		glad to say	
as a result		glad to see	
at a loss		I should like to have	
at a time		I should like to know	
at such a time		in a few days	
bill of sale		in a few months	
by the way		in addition to the	
during the last		in addition to this	
during the past		in order to be	
for a few days		in order to become	
for a few minutes		in relation to the	
for a long time		in such a manner	
for a minute		in the market	
for a moment		in the past	
glad to have		in the world	
glad to know		line of business	

line of goods		out of the	
line of work		out of them	
many of the		out of this	
many of them		out of town	
men and women		should like to have	
more and more		should like to see	
more or less		some of our	
none of the		some of the	
none of them		some of them	
on the market		some of these	
one of our		some of this	
one of the		some of those	
one of the best		son-in-law	
one of the most		such a thing	
one of them		two or three	
one of these		up and down	
one of those		up to date	
one or two		we should like to have	
ought to have		week or two	
out of date		will you please	
out of that			

Understand, understood

actually understand

better understand

better understanding

easily understand

friendly understanding

has understood

I could understand

I do not understand

I understand

it is understood

misunderstanding

misunderstood

mutual understanding

my understanding

please understand

readily understand

to understand

we cannot understand

we hope you will understand

we understand

we understand that

with the understanding

you can understand

you do not understand

you will understand

LESSON 44

Compound words

anybody

anyhow

anything

anywhere

everybody

everyone

everything

everywhere

hereafter

heretofore

however

nobody

notwithstanding

somebody

someone

somewhere

Thanksgiving

whatsoever

whensoever   whomsoever   within

wheresoever   whosoever   withstand

LESSON 45

Brief forms

acknowledge	publication	regular
acknowledged	publications	regularly
acknowledgment	publish	situation
estate	published	state
future	publishers	stated
never	quantities	statement
public	quantity	states

Phrases

in the future   in this state   to publish

Phrases

per gallon   per hundredweight   per pound

LESSON 46

Brief forms

allow	corrected	envelopes
allowance	correction	experience
allowed	correctly	experienced
correct	envelope	experiences

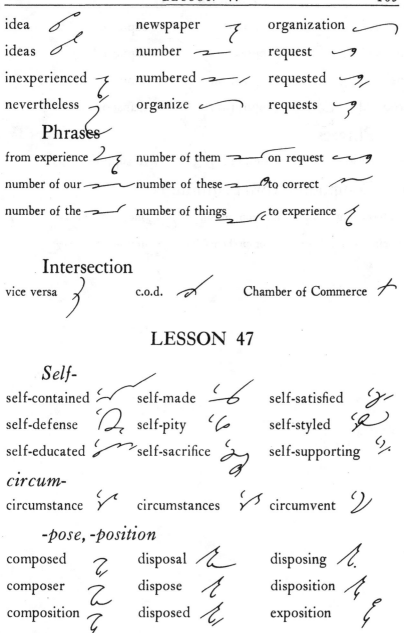

idea   newspaper   organization

ideas   number   request

inexperienced numbered   requested

nevertheless   organize   requests

Phrases

from experience   number of them   on request

number of our   number of these   to correct

number of the   number of things   to experience

Intersection

vice versa   c.o.d.   Chamber of Commerce

LESSON 47

Self-

self-contained   self-made   self-satisfied

self-defense   self-pity   self-styled

self-educated   self-sacrifice self-supporting

circum-

circumstance   circumstances   circumvent

-pose, -position

composed   disposal   disposing

composer   dispose   disposition

composition   disposed   exposition

imposed	proposed	suppose
opposed	proposes	supposed
position	proposition	supposition
proposal	propositions	transposition

Phrases

| in a position | I suppose | to suppose |

Compound word beginnings

| unenterprising | uncompromising | uncontrollable |
| disinclination | incomprehensible | uninsured |

CHAPTER IX

LESSON 49

Brief forms

agent	discovered	regard
agents	immediate	regards
between	immediately	throughout
cover	opinion	valuation
covered	question	value
covers	questions	valued

Phrases

between the	I am of the opinion	throughout the
between these	in our opinion	throughout this
between this	in question	to cover
between us	in regard	to value
between your	out of the question	we are of the opinion
		with regard

-ings

bearings	buildings	clippings
beginnings	casings	earnings

drawings	holdings	pleadings
evenings	linings	proceedings
feelings	offerings	savings
fittings	meetings	servings
furnishings	openings	things
hearings	paintings	

-ingly

accordingly	increasingly	seemingly
exceedingly	approvingly	unknowingly

Phrases

in this morning's	so many things	such things
many things	Friday mornings	this morning's

LESSON 50

Brief forms

conclude	house	particularly
concluded	household	particulars
conclusion	houses	subject
conclusive	object	success
confidence	objection	successes
confident	particular	warehouse

Phrases

in particular	on the subject	in conclusion

-sume, -sumption

assume	consume	presume
assumed	consumed	presumed
assumes	consumer	presumptive
assuming	consuming	resume
assumption	presumably	resumed

-ulate

accumulate	circulating	speculation
accumulated	circulation	stimulate
accumulation	congratulate	stimulated
calculate	congratulations	stimulates
circulated	population	tabulation

Phrases

I presume   I presume that   to calculate

LESSON 51

Brief forms

advantage	directed	railroad
advantages	direction	railroads
correspond	directly	recognize
correspondence	director	recognized
corresponding	directors	refer
direct	enough	reference

| referred | ✓ | refers | ✓ | wondering | ∾ |
| referring | ✓ | wonder | ∾ | yesterday | ℘ |

Phrases

| good enough | ⌐ | to which you refer | ✓ | with reference | ✓ |
| I wonder | ∾ | we directed | ✓ | with reference to the | ✓ |

-less

doubtless	✓	hopeless	ℓ	unless	⌐
helpless	ℓ	needless	✓	worthless	∾
uselessly	✓	helplessness	ℓ	heartless	ℓ

LESSON 52

Brief forms

automobile	✓	etc.	✓	likewise	✓
character	✓	govern	⌐	otherwise	✓
characters	✓	government	⌐	prosecute	✓
circle	✓	instance	✓	prosecution	✓
circular	✓	instant	✓	remainder	✓

Phrases

| for instance | ✓ | to govern | ⌐ | in this instance | ✓ |
| | | | | to prosecute | ✓ |

Geographical terminations

-burg

Pittsburgh   Newburgh   Fitchburg

Harrisonburg   Plattsburg   Greensburg

-ville

Jacksonville   Evansville   Brownsville

Gainesville   Louisville   Coatesville

Knoxville   Nashville   Zanesville

-field

Winfield   Pittsfield   Bloomfield

Mansfield   Springfield   Plainfield

-port

Bridgeport   Newport   Gulfport

Westport   Logansport   Glassport

LESSON 53

Geographical terminations

-ford

Stamford   Bedford   Medford

Rockford   Hartford   Bradford

-ington

Torrington   Washington   Lexington

Bloomington   Burlington   Arlington

Huntington   Irvington   Wilmington

-ingham

Framingham   Cunningham   Buckingham

-ton

Evanston   Princeton   Cranston

-town

Morristown   Norristown   Tarrytown

Allentown   Lewistown   Jamestown

Phrases

New York, New York   Buffalo, New York

Chicago, Illinois   San Francisco, California

St. Louis, Missouri   Boston, Massachusetts

Rochester, New York

INDEX TO WORDS

(Note: *a, 3* means that the word may first be written in Lesson 3, in *Gregg Short-hand Simplified.*)

a, 3
abandon, 31
ability, 29
able, 2
abnormal, 6
about, 14
above, 13
abroad, 4
absence, 18
absent, 21
absolute, 22
absorb, 4
abstract, 33
accept, 18
acceptable, 23
acceptance, 31
accepted, 20
access, 5
accident, 31
accommodate, 37
accommodation, 41
accompanied, 17
accomplish, 37
accomplished, 37
accordance, 17
accordingly, 49
account, 23
accountant, 23
accounted, 23
accrued, 13
accumulate, 50
accumulated, 50
accumulation, 50
accurate, 6
accusation, 39
accuse, 39
accustomed, 31
acknowledge, 45
acknowledged, 45
acknowledgment, 45
acquainted, 21
acquire, 40
acquirement, 40
act, 33
acted, 33
action, 8
active, 33
actively, 33
activity, 33
acts, 33
actual, 10
actually, 10
acute, 19
adaptable, 23
adapted, 20
add, 3
added, 20
adding, 6
addition, 41
additional, 41
address, 18
addresses, 5
adequate, 39
adhere, 6
adjust, 18
adjustable, 23
adjusted, 20
adjustment, 23

adjusts, 18
administer, 20
admission, 41
admit, 6
admitted, 20
adopt, 4
adopted, 20
adult, 38
advance, 18
advances, 5
advantage, 51
advantages, 51
advertise, 34
advertisement, 34
advice, 3
advices, 5
advisability, 29
advisable, 23
advocate, 39
affect, 33
affected, 33
affects, 33
affix, 5
afford, 38
after, 11
aftermath, 25
afternoon, 25
afterthought, 25
afterward, 38
again, 6
against, 33
age, 2
agencies, 18
agent, 49
agents, 49
aggregate, 39
aging, 6
ago, 3
agree, 3
agreeable, 23
agreement, 23
agriculture, 38
ahead, 15
aid, 1
aim, 1
aiming, 3
alarm, 3
algebra, 41
all, 11
Allentown, 53
allocation, 39
allotment, 23
allow, 46
allowance, 46
allowed, 46
almost, 38
alone, 6
along, 17
aloud, 19
alphabet, 41
alphabetical, 41
already, 38
also, 38
alter, 38
alterations, 38
alternate, 38
alternatives, 38
although, 38

altogether, 38
aluminum, 20
always, 20
am, 3
ambitious, 18
amend, 34
amended, 34
amendment, 34
among, 17
amount, 23
amounted, 23
amounting, 23
amounts, 23
ample, 6
amplifier, 29
amplify, 29
amply, 9
an, 3
analysis, 5
analytical, 25
anchor, 16
ancient, 8
and, 11
angle, 16
ankle, 16
announce, 23
announced, 23
announcement, 23
announces, 23
annoyance, 10
annoyed, 10
annual, 18
annually, 18
annum, 18
another, 14
answer, 18
answered, 17
anticipate, 21
anticipated, 21
anticipation, 21
antique, 21
anxious, 18
anxiously, 18
any, 20
anybody, 44
anyhow, 44
anyone, 20
anything, 20
anywhere, 44
apiece, 18
apologies, 40
apologize, 40
apology, 40
apparatus, 13
apparent, 21
appeal, 6
appear, 3
appeared, 17
appendicitis, 40
appendix, 26
appliance, 11
applicable, 23
applicant, 21
application, 8
applies, 18
apply, 6
appointed, 21
appointment, 23

appreciable, 23
appreciate, 11
appreciated, 20
appreciation, 11
appreciative, 26
approach, 23
approached, 23
appropriate, 23
appropriation, 23
approval, 23
approve, 23
approved, 23
approvingly, 49
approximate, 23
April, 22
apron, 23
aptitude, 39
are, 3
area, 11
areas, 11
argue, 19
arisen, 18
arises, 5
arithmetic, 41
Arlington, 53
arm, 3
arms, 18
army, 3
around, 23
arrange, 6
arrangement, 23
arrive, 3
arrives, 18
art, 6
article, 25
artist, 33
as, 18
ascertain, 31
ashamed, 21
aside, 11
ask, 18
asserted, 20
assessed, 5
assessment, 23
assets, 18
assigned, 21
assignment, 23
assist, 33
assistance, 33
assistant, 33
association, 11
assorted, 32
assortment, 32
assume, 50
assumed, 50
assumes, 50
assuming, 50
assumption, 50
assurance, 18
assure, 18
assured, 17
assures, 18
astray, 8
at, 3
ate, 1
Atlantic, 40
attached, 6
attainment, 31

113

attempt, 31
attempted, 31
attempting, 31
attend, 31
attendance, 31
attended, 31
attention, 31
attested, 33
attitude, 39
attorney, 32
attractive, 33
attribute, 40
audience, 31
audit, 20
auditor, 20
auditorium, 22
August, 22
aunt, 21
auspices, 5
authentic, 40
author, 6
authoritative, 26
authorities, 29
authorization, 8
auto, 4
automatic, 31
automatically, 31
automobile, 52
available, 23
avenue, 22
average, 3
avoid, 10
await, 15
awaited, 20
awaiting, 15
awake, 15
award, 17
awarded, 17
aware, 15
away, 15
awful, 29
awkward, 38
awkwardly, 38
back, 6
background, 23
backs, 18
backward, 38
bacteria, 11
bad, 6
badly, 9
bag, 6
baggage, 6
bags, 18
balance, 18
balances, 5
ball, 6
band, 21
bank, 16
banker, 16
bankruptcy, 16
banquet, 16
barely, 9
bargain, 3
barrel, 6
base, 2
baseball, 6
basement, 23
bases, 5
basis, 5
basket, 18
bath, 3
battery, 6
be, 4
bear, 6
bearing, 3
bearings, 49
beautiful, 29
beautify, 29
became, 10
because, 10

become, 16
bed, 3
Bedford, 53
been, 9
before, 4
beg, 6
began, 10
begin, 10
beginning, 10
beginnings, 49
begins, 10
begun, 16
behalf, 10
behind, 21
belief, 16
believe, 16
believer, 16
belong, 17
below, 10
belt, 6
beneficial, 8
beneficiary, 11
benefit, 6
benefited, 20
bent, 21
besides, 11
best, 33
betray, 10
better, 2
between, 49
beyond, 21
bias, 11
bid, 6
bids, 3
big, 21
bigger, 21
bigness, 21
billed, 17
billing, 11
bills, 11
bind, 21
binder, 21
bindery, 21
biology, 40
bird, 17
birth, 3
birthday, 3
black, 6
blacksmith, 6
blame, 2
blank, 16
blanket, 16
block, 4
blood, 13
Bloomfield, 52
Bloomington 53
blotter, 4
blouse, 19
blue, 13
blunder, 21
board, 17
boats, 2
body, 34
boiled, 17
boiler, 10
bolt, 6
bond, 21
bonded, 21
bone, 6
bonus, 18
book, 13
booked, 13
bookkeeping, 17
booklet, 14
booth, 13
boots, 13
border, 17
born, 6,
borrow, 6
borrowers, 6

both, 6
bother, 14
bothered, 14
bottom, 31
bought, 4
bound, 34
bouquet, 13
bow, 19
box, 5
boxed, 5
boxes, 5
boy, 10
boyhood, 38
boys, 10
braces, 5
Bradford, 53
branch, 6
branches, 18
brand, 21
bread, 6
break, 6
bridge, 6
Bridgeport, 52
bridges, 18
brief, 2
briefly, 9
bright, 6
brilliant, 21
bring, 16
broad, 4
broadcasting, 4
broader, 4
Broadway, 15
broke, 2
bronze, 4
brother, 14
brought, 4
brown, 23
Brownsville, 52
brush, 16
brushed, 16
Buckingham, 53
bud, 13
budget, 16
build, 17
builders, 17
buildings, 49
built, 6
bulbs, 13
bulk, 13
bulletin, 31
bumper, 16
bunch, 16
bundles, 34
burden, 17
bureau, 19
Burlington, 53
burned, 21
bus, 18
bushel, 13
business, 11
businesses, 11
businesslike, 11
busy, 18
but, 4
butter, 13
button, 31
buy, 2
buyer, 6
by, 4
cabinet, 6
cable, 23
cablegram, 29
calculate, 50
calendar, 21
call, 6
called, 17
came, 2
campaign, 6
can, 3

cancel, 18
canceled, 17
cancellation, 8
candy, 21
canned, 21
cannot, 3
can't, 3
capable, 23
capacity, 18
capital, 3
car, 6
card, 17
care, 6
careful, 29
carefully, 29
cargo, 6
carload, 6
carpenter, 26
carry, 6
carton, 31
case, 18
casement, 23
cases, 5
cash, 6
cashier, 6
casings, 49
cast, 18
casting, 3
casually, 18
casualty, 29
catalogue, 4
catch, 6
caught, 4
cause, 4
caused, 4
causes, 5
caution, 8
cave, 6
cement, 20
census, 5
cent, 21
center, 21
central, 21
centralized, 21
century, 21
certain, 31
certainly, 31
certainty, 31
certificate, 39
certified, 29
certify, 29
chain, 6
chains, 2
chair, 6
chairman, 6
chance, 18
chances, 5
changed, 2
changes, 18
character, 52
characters, 52
charge, 6
charged, 3
charges, 18
charity, 29
charming, 3
cheap, 6
cheaper, 2
cheapest, 33
check, 3
checks, 18
cheese, 18
chemical, 25
chemicals, 25
chemistry, 33
chest, 18
chickens, 3
chief, 6
child, 17
childhood, 38

114

children, 17
choice, 10
choose, 18
chorus, 13
chose, 2
chosen, 18
Christmas, 18
church, 3
cigars, 18
circle, 52
circular, 52
circulated, 50
circulating, 50
circulation, 50
circumstance, 47
circumstances, 47
circumvent, 47
city, 18
claim, 2
claimed, 21
claims, 18
clarity, 29
class, 18
classes, 5
classification, 29
classified, 29
clause, 4
clauses, 5
clean, 6
cleaned, 21
clear, 2
clearer, 6
clearly, 9
clerk, 6
clerks, 18
client, 21
clipping, 6
clippings, 49
clock, 4
close, 2
closely, 9
closes, 5
closest, 33
clothing, 6
clutch, 16
coal, 6
coast, 18
Coatesville, 52
cogent, 26
coil, 10
coin, 10
cold, 17
collar, 6
collect, 33
collected, 33
collection, 8
college, 6
collision, 8
color, 13
colored, 17
column, 16
combination, 41
combine, 37
come, 16
comedian, 37
comedies, 37
command, 37
commence, 37
commend, 37
commendation, 41
comment, 37
commerce, 37
commercial, 37
commission, 41
commissioner, 41
commitments, 37
committed, 37
committee, 37
commodities, 37
commodity, 37

common, 37
commonly, 37
communicate, 39
communication, 39
communities, 37
community, 37
compact, 37
companies, 17
companion, 37
company, 17
comparative, 37
compare, 37
compared, 37
comparison, 37
compel, 37
compelled, 37
compensation, 37
compete, 37
competent, 37
competition, 41
competitive, 37
competitor, 37
competitors, 37
compiled, 37
complaint, 37
complete, 37
completed, 37
completely, 37
completion, 37
compliance, 37
compliment, 37
complimentary, 37
comply, 37
composed, 47
composer, 47
composition, 47
compound, 37
comprehensive, 37
compressor, 37
concealed, 37
concentrate, 37
conception, 37
concern, 37
concerned, 37
concerns, 37
concert, 37
concession, 37
conclude, 50
concluded, 50
conclusion, 50
conclusive, 50
concrete, 37
condense, 37
condensed, 37
condition, 41
conduct, 37
conducted, 37
conductor, 37
confer, 37
conference, 37
confess, 37
confidence, 50
confident, 50
confidential, 37
confine, 37
confined, 37
confirm, 37
confirmation, 41
confirmed, 37
confiscate, 39
confiscation, 39
conflict, 37
confuse, 39
confused, 39
confusing, 39
confusion, 39
congested, 37
congestion, 37
congratulate, 50
congratulations, 50

conjunction, 37
connected, 37
connection, 37
connections, 37
conscientious, 37
consent, 37
consequently, 10
conservative, 37
consider, 34
considerably, 34
consideration, 34
considered, 34
consign, 37
consigned, 37
consignee, 37
consignment, 37
consist, 37
consisted, 37
consistent, 37
consistently, 37
consists, 37
consolidate, 37
consolidation, 41
constant, 37
constantly, 37
constitute, 40
construct, 37
constructed, 37
construction, 37
constructive, 37
consult, 38
consultation, 41
consulted, 38
consume, 50
consumed, 50
consumer, 50
consuming, 50
contact, 37
contain, 37
contained, 37
container, 37
contemplate, 37
contemplated, 37
content, 37
contention, 37
contest, 37
continent, 37
contingent, 37
continuance, 37
continue, 37
continued, 37
continues, 37
continuous, 37
contract, 37
contracted, 37
contractor, 37
contracts, 37
contrary, 37
contrast, 37
contribute, 37
contributed, 40
contribution, 40
control, 37
controversy, 37
convenience, 41
convenient, 41
conveniently, 41
convention, 37
conversation, 37
conversion, 37
convert, 37
converted, 37
convey, 37
convince, 37
cook, 13
cooker, 13
cool, 13
co-operate, 4
co-operated, 20

co-operation, 8
co-operative, 26
copies, 4
copper, 4
cord, 17
cordial, 6
cordially, 9
corduroy, 17
corn, 6
corner, 6
corporation, 8
correct, 46
corrected, 46
correction, 46
correctly, 46
correspond, 51
correspondence, 51
corresponding, 51
corrugated, 39
cost, 33
costing, 33
costly, 33
costs, 33
cottage, 4
cotton, 31
could, 4
council, 23
counsel, 23
count, 23
counted, 23
counter, 23
counting, 23
country, 21
county, 23
couple, 13
coupon, 13
course, 6
courses, 5
court, 32
courteous, 22
courtesy, 18
cover, 49
covered, 49
covers, 49
cow, 19
cracked, 6
crank, 16
Cranston, 53
cream, 2
create, 11
created, 20
creative, 26
credit, 20
credited, 20
credits, 20
cried, 2
critical, 25
criticism, 5
crop, 4
cross, 4
crossed, 4
crowd, 19
crown, 23
crude, 13
crushed, 16
cry, 6
cubic, 19
culminate, 38
culture, 38
Cunningham, 53
cup, 13
cups, 13
cure, 19
currency, 18
current, 21
curriculum, 41
curtain, 31
custom, 31
customary, 31
customer, 31

115

cut, 13
cylinder, 21
daily, 9
damage, 31
damaged, 31
danger, 31
dark, 6
data, 6
date, 21
dated, 21
dates, 21
daughter, 4
day, 1
days, 2
dead, 20
deal, 1
dealer, 1
dear, 1
Dear Sir, 7
Dear Sirs, 7
death, 6
debit, 10
debt, 20
debtor, 20
decay, 12
December, 22
decide, 11
decided, 11
decidedly, 11
decision, 12
declaration, 8
declare, 12
decline, 6
decrease, 18
deduct, 33
deducted, 33
deduction, 20
deductions, 20
deed, 1
deemed, 21
deep, 6
deeply, 9
defect, 33
defense, 26
defer, 26
deferred, 26
defiance, 26
definite, 26
defy, 26
delay, 12
dalayed, 12
delays, 10
deliberate, 10
delighted, 20
delightful, 29
delinquent, 40
deliver, 16
delivered, 16
deliveries, 16
demand, 34
demonstrate, 31
demonstration, 31
deny, 31
departing, 34
depend, 26
dependable, 26
depended, 26
dependent, 26
depends, 26
depleted, 20
deportment, 32
deposit, 12
deposited, 20
depositor, 12
depository, 12
deposits, 10
depot, 10
depreciation, 11
derive, 10
describe, 10

description, 10
descriptive, 26
deserve, 12
design, 12
designed, 21
designer, 12
desirable, 23
desire, 7
desired, 8
desires, 7
desirous, 18
desk, 18
despite, 10
destination, 41
destined, 31
destroy, 10
detail, 20
detailed, 20
detained, 31
determine, 32
determined, 32
develop, 26
developed, 26
development, 26
develops, 26
device, 26
devise, 26
devised, 26
devote, 26
devoted, 26
diagnosis, 11
diagram, 29
dial, 11
diameter, 11
diamond, 34
dictate, 6
did, 21
die, 6
diet, 11
differ, 26
difference, 26
different, 26
difficult, 32
difficulty, 32
dig, 6
diligently, 26
dimensions, 31
dinner, 31
direct, 51
directed, 51
direction, 51
directly, 51
director, 51
directors, 51
disability, 29
disappoint, 21
disastrous, 13
disbursed, 10
disclose, 10
discontinue, 37
discontinued, 37
discount, 23
discounted, 23
discouraged, 10
discovered, 49
discrepancy, 10
discretion, 10
discrimination, 41
discuss, 18
discussed, 18
discussion, 13
disease, 10
dishes, 18
disinclination, 47
dismiss, 10
dismissal, 10
dispatch, 10
display, 10
disposal, 47
dispose, 47

disposed, 47
disposing, 47
disposition, 47
dispute, 19
dissolved, 10
distance, 31
distribute, 40
distributed, 40
distribution, 40
distributors, 40
district, 33
ditches, 18
ditto, 20
diversified, 29
diversion, 26
divert, 6
diverted, 26
divide, 26
divided, 26
dividend, 34
division, 26
do, 13
dock, 4
doctor, 16
document, 23
does, 13
dog, 4
dollar, 6
domestic, 31
donation, 41
done, 16
door, 6
double, 23
doubt, 19
doubted, 20
doubtful, 29
doubtless, 51
down, 23
draft, 6
drag, 6
drain, 1
drastic, 18
draw, 4
drawee, 11
drawer, 6
drawings, 49
drawn, 6
drew, 13
drier, 11
drill, 3
drilled, 17
drinking, 16
drive, 2
driver, 6
drop, 4
drove, 1
drug, 13
drum, 16
dry, 2
duck, 13
due, 22
dues, 22
dug, 13
duly, 22
duplicate, 39
duplicated, 39
duplication, 39
during, 16
dust, 13
duty, 22
dwelling, 15
dye, 2
each, 2
earlier, 9
earliest, 33
early, 9
earn, 3
earned, 21
earnest, 33
earnestly, 33

earnings, 49
earth, 6
easiest, 33
easily, 9
east, 1
Easter, 1
eastern, 32
easy, 1
eccentric, 21
edges, 6
edification, 29
edition, 41
editor, 20
editorial, 20
education, 39
educational, 39
effect, 33
effective, 33
efficiency, 8
efficient, 8
effort, 38
efforts, 38
either, 14
elastic, 18
elect, 33
election, 8
electric, 27
electric wire, 27
electrical, 27
electrically, 27
electrician, 27
electricity, 27
electronics, 27
electros, 27
electrotype, 27
elementary, 23
elements, 23
eligible, 23
eliminate, 20
eloquent, 40
else, 34
elsewhere, 34
embarrass, 37
embarrassment, 37
embraces, 37
emphasis, 37
emphatically, 37
empire, 37
employed, 37
employees, 37
employment, 37
emptied, 21
empty, 21
enable, 26
enamel, 6
enclose, 14
enclosed, 14
enclosure, 14
encountered, 37
encourage, 37
encouraged, 37
encouragement, 37
encroachment, 37
end, 11
endeavor, 37
endorse, 21
endorsed, 21
endorsement, 23
endorser, 21
engage, 37
engaged, 37
engagement, 37
engine, 37
engineer, 37
engineers, 37
engrave, 37
engraver, 37
enjoy, 37
enjoyed, 37
enlarge, 37
enormous, 18
enough, 51

116

enrolled, 37
en route, 37
enter, 27
entered, 27
entering, 27
enterprise, 27
entertain, 31
entertainment, 31
enthusiasm, 37
enthusiastic, 37
entire, 21
entirely, 21
entitled, 21
entrance, 27
entrances, 27
entry, 21
enumerated, 22
envelope, 46
envelopes, 46
equal, 10
equally, 10
equip, 15
equipment, 23
equipped, 15
equitable, 23
equivalent, 41
eradication, 39
erroneous, 22
error, 6
errors, 18
especially, 9
esquire, 40
essential, 8
essentially, 9
essentials, 8
establishing, 18
establishment, 23
estate, 45
esteemed, 31
estimate, 31
estimated, 31
estimation, 41
etc., 52
eternal, 32
Evanston, 53
Evansville, 52
even, 1
evening, 3
evenings, 49
event, 21
eventually, 21
ever, 19
every, 19
everybody, 44
everyone, 44
everything, 44
everywhere, 44
evidence, 31
evident, 31
evidently, 31
exact, 33
exactly, 33
examination, 41
examine, 20
examined, 20
examiner, 20
example, 7
exceed, 7
exceeding, 7
exceedingly, 49
excellent, 21
except, 7
exception, 8
exceptionally, 9
excess, 7
excessive, 7
excessively, 9
exchange, 7
excited, 20
exclude, 13
exclusive, 13

excuse, 39
excuses, 39
executed, 20
executive, 26
exempt, 21
exemption, 8
exhaust, 33
exhausted, 33
exhibit, 7
exhibited, 20
exhibition, 8
exist, 33
existed, 33
existence, 33
exists, 33
expansion, 8
expect, 33
expected, 33
expects, 33
expedite, 7
expend, 26
expended, 26
expenditure, 26
expense, 7
expenses, 7
expensive, 7
experience, 46
experienced, 46
experiences, 46
experiment, 23
experimental, 23
expert, 7
expiration, 8
expire, 7
expired, 17
expires, 7
explain, 7
explained, 21
explains, 7
explanation, 41
export, 32
exposition, 47
express, 7
expressed, 7
expression, 8
extend, 34
extended, 34
extends, 34
extension, 31
extensive, 31
extensively, 31
extent, 31
exterior, 7
external, 32
extra, 7
extraordinary, 32
extras, 7
extreme, 7
extremely, 9
fabric, 6
face, 1
faced, 1
faces, 5
facilitate, 18
facilities, 29
facility, 29
fact, 33
factory, 6
facts, 33
faculty, 29
fail, 1
failed, 17
fails, 18
failure, 10
fair, 1
fairly, 9
faith, 6
faithful, 29
fall, 6
famed, 21
familiar, 3

families, 9
family, 9
famous, 18
far, 3
farm, 6
farms, 3
farther, 14
fashion, 8
fast, 3
fastened, 21
father, 14
fault, 6
favor, 1
favorable, 23
favorably, 9
favored, 17
favors, 18
feasible, 23
feather, 14
feature, 10
February, 22
federal, 6
fee, 1
feed, 1
feel, 1
feelings, 49
feels, 18
fees, 1
feet, 1
fell, 6
fellow, 3
fellows, 18
fellowship, 25
few, 19
fewer, 19
fiber, 6
field, 17
file, 6
filed, 17
files, 2
fill, 6
filled, 17
final, 6
finally, 9
finance, 18
finances, 5
financial, 8
financially, 9
find, 21
finest, 33
finish, 6
fireproofing, 23
firm, 6
firmly, 9
firms, 3
first, 33
fiscal, 18
fit, 6
Fitchburg, 52
fitted, 20
fittings, 49
fix, 5
fixed, 5
fixes, 5
fixtures, 18
flag, 6
flat, 6
flax, 5
flexible, 23
floor, 6
flour, 19
flowers, 19
flush, 16
foe, 1
fold, 17
folded, 17
folder, 17
follow, 6
food, 13
foot, 13
for, 4
force, 38

forced, 38
foreclosure, 38
foreign, 6
foreman, 38
forerunner, 38
forget, 38
form, 38
formal, 38
former, 38
formerly, 38
forms, 38
forth, 38
fortitude, 39
fortune, 38
forward, 38
forwarded, 38
found, 23
foundation, 41
foundry, 23
fountain, 31
fourth, 38
framed, 21
frames, 18
Framingham, 53
frank, 16
frankly, 16
frantic, 40
fraternity, 32
free, 1
freedom, 31
freely, 9
freight, 1
frequent, 40
frequently, 40
fresh, 6
freshmen, 20
Friday, 22
friend, 21
from, 9
front, 21
frozen, 18
fruit, 13
fuel, 19
full, 13
fully, 13
fumed, 21
fun, 16
functions, 16
fund, 21
fundamental, 23
fur, 6
furlough, 38
furnace, 38
furnaces, 38
furnish, 38
furnished, 38
furnishing, 38
furnishings, 49
furniture, 38
further, 38
furthermore, 38
future, 45
gain, 2
gained, 21
Gainesville, 52
gallon, 6
game, 2
garden, 17
garment, 23
gas, 18
gasoline, 18
gather, 14
gauge, 6
gave, 2
gay, 6
gear, 6
general, 21
generally, 21
genteel, 26
gentle, 26
gentlemen, 26

genuine, 22
geographical, 25
get, 6
getting, 3
gift, 6
girls, 2
give, 6
given, 3
gives, 18
glad, 14
gladly, 14
glance, 18
glass, 18
glasses, 5
Glassport, 52
glued, 13
go, 3
goes, 3
going, 3
gold, 17
golden, 17
golf, 6
gone, 20
good, 3
goods, 3
got, 21
gotten, 31
govern, 52
government, 52
grade, 2
graded, 20
grades, 18
grading, 3
gradual, 18
gradually, 18
graduate, 22
graduation, 22
grand, 21
grant, 21
granted, 21
graphs, 18
grateful, 29
gratified, 29
gratifying, 29
gratitude, 39
gray, 6
great, 17
greater, 17
greatest, 33
greatly, 17
green, 6
Greensburg, 52
greeting, 3
grew, 13
grind, 21
grocery, 18
gross, 18
ground, 23
group, 13
grouped, 13
grow, 2
grown, 6
growth, 6
guarantee, 21
guard, 17
guess, 18
guidance, 31
guide, 6
guided, 20
guilty, 6
Gulfport, 52
gummed, 21
gun, 16
habit, 3
had, 6
hair, 1
half, 6
hand, 11
handed, 11
handkerchief, 16
handled, 17
hanger, 16

happen, 6
happened, 26
happens, 18
happy, 6
hard, 17
harder, 17
hardihood, 38
hardly, 17
hardship, 25
hardware, 17
harm, 3
harmony, 20
Harrisonburg, 52
Hartford, 53
harvest, 33
has, 3
haste, 1
hasten, 1
hate, 1
hats, 18
hauled, 17
have, 4
hazard, 17
he, 3
head, 6
headed, 20
headquarters, 32
heads, 18
health, 6
healthy, 3
hear, 1
heard, 17
hearings, 49
heartily, 9
heartless, 51
heat, 1
heater, 1
heating, 3
heavily, 9
heavy, 6
heed, 1,
height, 2
held, 17
help, 6
helped, 3
helpful, 29
helpfulness, 29
helpless, 51
helplessness, 51
helps, 18
her, 3
hereafter, 44
hereto, 7
heretofore, 44
herewith, 4
herself, 25
hesitancy, 31
hesitation, 41
hide, 2
highest, 33
highly, 9
highway, 13
him, 3
himself, 25
hinges, 18
hints, 21
hired, 17
his, 4
historical, 25
hit, 6
hoist, 10
hold, 17
holders, 17
holdings, 49
holds, 17
hole, 6
holiday, 6
home, 6
homes, 6
homes, 18
homestead, 20

honest, 33
honestly, 33
honesty, 33
honor, 6
hook, 13
hop, 4
hope, 2
hopeful, 29
hopeless, 51
horn, 6
horses, 6
hosiery, 6
hospital, 4
hot, 4
hotel, 6
hour, 3
hours, 3
house, 50
household, 50
houses, 50
hesitated, 20
how, 19
however, 44
human, 20
hung, 16
hunting, 21
Huntington, 53
hurry, 3
hurt, 3
I, 3
idea, 46
ideal, 22
ideas, 46
identical, 31
identically, 31
identification, 31
identified, 31
identify, 31
if, 6
ignore, 6
ignored, 17
illness, 18
illustrate, 13
illustrated, 20
illustration, 8
illustrations, 13
imagine, 6
imitation, 41
immediate, 49
immediately, 49
immensely, 20
immodest, 37
immoral, 37
immortal, 37
impairment, 37
impartial, 37
imperative, 37
implements, 37
import, 37
importance, 19
important, 19
imported, 37
imports, 37
imposed, 47
impossible, 37
impracticable, 37
impress, 37
impressed, 37
impression, 37
imprint, 37
imprinted, 37
imprinting, 37
improper, 37
improved, 37
improvement, 37
in, 3
inability, 29
inactive, 33
inadequate, 39
inadvisable, 23
incapable, 37
incentive, 37

inch, 37
incident, 37
incidental, 37
incidentally, 37
inclement, 35
inclined, 35
include, 35
included, 35
includes, 35
inclusive, 35
income, 37
incomprehensible, 47
inconvenience, 41
inconvenienced, 41
inconvenient, 41
incorporated, 37
increase, 37
increased, 37
increases, 37
increasingly, 49
incurred, 37
indebted, 37
indebtedness, 37
indeed, 37
indemnity, 37
index, 21
indexes, 21
indicate, 39
indicated, 39
indicates, 39
indication, 39
individual, 21
induce, 22
inducement, 23
industry, 21
inevitably, 9
inexcusable, 39
inexpensive, 7
inexperienced, 46
infants, 37
infer, 37
inferior, 37
inferred, 37
influence, 37
inform, 38
information, 41
informed, 38
initial, 8
initialed, 8
initiative, 26
injured, 37
injuries, 37
injury, 37
ink, 16
inlaid, 37
inquire, 40
inquiries, 40
inquiry, 40
insert, 37
inserted, 37
insertion, 37
inside, 37
insist, 37
insisted, 37
inspection, 37
inspiration, 37
install, 37
installation, 37
installed, 37
installment, 37
instance, 52
instant, 52
instead, 37
institute, 40
institution, 40
instruct, 37
instructed, 37
instruction, 37
instructor, 37
instructive, 37
instrument, 37
insurance, 37

118

insure, 37
insured, 37
intact, 33
intelligence, 21
intelligent, 26
intelligently, 26
intend, 37
intended, 37
intends, 37
intention, 37
interest, 33
interested, 33
interesting, 33
interests, 33
interfere, 27
interference, 27
interim, 27
interior, 27
intermediate, 27
internal, 27
international, 27
interpretation, 41
interpreted, 27
interrupted, 27
interruption, 27
interval, 27
interview, 27
intimate, 37
intimated, 37
into, 21
introduce, 27
introduced, 27
introduction, 27
invariably, 27
inventory, 37
invest, 37
invested, 37
investigate, 39
investigation, 39
investment, 37
invitation, 41
invite, 37
invited, 37
invoice, 37
invoiced, 37
invoices, 37
involved, 37
iron, 2
irrigation, 39
Irvington, 53
is, 4
island, 21
issue, 22
issued, 22
issues, 22
it, 3
item, 31
itemized, 31
itinerary, 31
its, 3
itself, 25
Jacksonville, 52
jam, 6
Jamestown, 53
jammed, 21
January, 22
jar, 6
jaw, 4
jelly, 6
jewel, 13
jewelers, 13
jewelry, 13
job, 4
jobber, 4
join, 10
joined, 21
joint, 21
jointly, 21
journal, 6
joy, 10
judge, 16

judgment, 23
July, 22
junction, 16
June, 22
juries, 18
jury, 18
just, 18
justice, 18
justification, 29
justified, 29
justify, 29
justly, 18
juvenile, 13
keep, 17
kept, 17
keys, 2
kill, 6
kind, 21
kindest, 33
kindness, 21
king, 16
kingdom, 31
kinship, 25
kitchen, 6
knee, 1
knew, 22
know, 1
knowledge, 6
known, 6
knows, 2
Knoxville, 52
label, 6
labor, 2
lack, 6
ladies, 18
lady, 6
lamps, 18
land, 21
lands, 21
language, 16
lantern, 32
large, 3
largely, 9
larger, 6
largest, 33
last, 33
lasting, 33
lasts, 33
late, 1
lately, 9
later, 1
latest, 33
lath, 3
lathe, 6
latitude, 39
laws, 4
lead, 1
learn, 6
learned, 21
lease, 18
leases, 5
leasing, 3
least, 2
leather, 14
leave, 1
lecture, 10
led, 3
ledger, 6
left, 6
leg, 6
legal, 6
legally, 9
legitimate, 31
lemon, 20
lend, 21
length, 16
lenses, 5
less, 18
lessons, 18
let, 14
letter, 4

letters, 14
Lewistown, 53
Lexington, 53
liabilities, 29
liable, 23
liberal, 6
liberty, 6
librarian, 11
library, 6
lieu, 22
life, 6
lifted, 20
light, 2
like, 9
likely, 9
likewise, 52
limited, 20
line, 6
lined, 21
lines, 18
lining, 3
linings, 49
link, 16
liquid, 15
liquidated, 20
list, 18
listed, 20
listen, 18
literatuure, 10
little, 3
live, 6
lives, 18
loaded, 20
loan, 6
loaned, 21
lobby, 4
locality, 29
locally, 9
locate, 39
located, 39
location, 39
lock, 4
locomotive, 26
Logansport, 52
logical, 25
logs, 4
long, 17
longer, 17
look, 13
looked, 13
loose, 13
lose, 13
loss, 4
losses, 5
lost, 4
lot, 4
loud, 19
Louisville, 52
low, 1
lower, 6
lowest, 33
loyal, 10
loyalty, 29
luck, 13
lumber, 16
lump, 16
lunch, 16
luncheon, 16
machine, 6
machines, 18
made, 1
magazine, 18
mail, 1
mailed, 17
main, 1
mainly, 9
maintain, 16
maintained, 31
maintenance, 31
major, 3
majority, 29

make, 6
makes, 18
making, 3
man, 6
manage, 20
management, 23
manager, 20
managers, 20
manhood, 38
manner, 20
Mansfield, 52
manual, 20
manufacture, 22
manufactured, 22
manufacturer, 22
manuscript, 22
many, 20
map, 6
maps, 18
March, 6
margin, 6
mark, 3
marked, 6
market, 7
marketed, 8
marks, 18
master, 3
match, 6
matches, 18
material, 6
materially, 9
matters, 19
mattresses, 5
mature, 18
maturity, 29
maximum, 20
may, 1
May, 22
me, 1
mean, 1
means, 2
meant, 20
meantime, 32
measure, 18
measurement, 23
measures, 18
meat, 1
mechanical, 25
mechanically, 25
medal, 3
Medford, 53
medical, 25
medicine, 18
medium, 31
meetings, 49
member, 20
membership, 25
memo, 20
memoranda, 41
memorandum, 41
memorandums, 41
memorial, 20
memory, 20
men, 20
mental, 20
mention, 20
mentioned, 20
merchanidse, 32
merchant, 32
merely, 9
merit, 6
messages, 18
met, 6
metal, 6
meter, 1
method, 6
middle, 3
might, 2
mighty, 6
mile, 6
milk, 6

119

mill, 6
milled, 17
millions, 22
mind, 34
mine, 6
mineral, 20
miniature, 20
minimum, 20
minute, 20
miscarry, 10
miscellaneous, 22
misfortune, 38
mislaid, 10
misleading, 10
misplaced, 10
miss, 18
mission, 8
mistake, 10
mistaken, 10
mix, 5
mixed, 5
mixer, 5
mob, 4,
model, 4
moderate, 4
modern, 32
modification, 29
modify, 29
moisture, 18
moment, 23
Monday, 22
monetary, 23
money, 20
monogram, 29
month, 20
monthly, 20
monument, 23
mop, 4
moral, 6
more, 3
morning, 21
Morristown, 53
mortal, 32
mortgage, 6
most, 11
mostly, 11
mother, 14
motion, 8
motive, 26
motor, 1
mount, 23
mountain, 31
mounted, 23
mouth, 19
move, 18
movement, 23
Mr., 7
Mrs., 11
much, 16
mud, 18
multiple, 38
multitude, 39
music, 22
musical, 25
muslin, 18
must, 7
mutual, 22
mutually, 22
my, 6
myself, 25
named, 21
namely, 9
names, 18
narrower, 6
Nashville, 52
national, 8
nationally, 9
native, 26
natural, 18
naturally, 18
nature, 18

navy, 1
near, 1
nearer, 1
nearest, 33
nearly, 9
neat, 1
necessarily, 16
necessary, 16
necessitate, 5
necessity, 5
need, 1
needed, 20
needless, 51
needs, 18
negative, 26
neglected, 33
neighborhood, 38
neighbors, 2
neither, 14
nervous, 18
net, 6
neuritis, 40
never, 45
nevertheless, 46
new, 22
Newburgh, 52
newer, 22
newest, 33
Newport, 52
news, 22
newspaper, 46
next, 16
nicely, 9
niece, 2
night, 2
no, 1
nobility, 29
nobody, 44
noise, 10
nominal, 20
none, 18
nonpayment, 23
noon, 18
nor, 6
normal, 6
normally, 9
Norristown, 53
north, 6
northern, 32
northwestern, 32
not, 3
notary, 1
notation, 41
note, 1
noted, 20
notes, 2
nothing, 14
notice, 18
notices, 5
notification, 29
notify, 29
notwithstanding, 44
November, 22
now, 19
nowhere, 17
number, 46
numbered, 46
numerous, 22
nurses, 5
nut, 18
object, 50
objection, 50
obligation, 39
oblige, 6
obliged, 2
observe, 4
obtain, 31
obtainable, 31
obtained, 31
obviate, 11
occasion, 8

occasionally, 9
occur, 4
occurred, 17
occurrence, 4
October, 22
of, 4
off, 4
offer, 4
offered, 17
offerings, 49
office, 21
officers, 21
offices, 21
official, 8
offset, 4
often, 4
oftener, 4
oil, 10
old, 17
older, 17
omission, 41
omit, 6
omitted, 20
on, 6
once, 19
one, 19
oneself, 25
only, 9
onward, 38
open, 2
opened, 26
openings, 49
operate, 4
operated, 20
operation, 8
opinion, 49
opportunity, 21
opposed, 47
opposite, 4
option, 8
or, 6
oral, 6
orange, 6
orchard, 17
order, 26
ordered, 26
orders, 26
ordinarily, 32
ordinary, 32
organ, 6
organization, 36
organize, 46
origin, 6
original, 6
originally, 9
ornamental, 23
other, 14
others, 14
otherwise, 52
ought, 4
ounce, 19
our, 3
ours, 3
ourselves, 25
out, 19
outline, 19
outlined, 21
outside, 19
outstanding, 32
oven, 13
over, 17
overburdened, 21
overcharge, 17
overdue, 22
overlooked, 17
oversight, 17
oversize, 17
owned, 21
owner, 6
ownership, 25
package, 6

packages, 18
page, 2
pages, 18
paid, 2
paint, 21
paintings, 49
pair, 6
paper, 2
paragraph, 6
parcel, 18
pardon, 17
parenthood, 38
parents, 21
park, 6
part, 34
partial, 8
participate, 34
particular, 50
particularly, 50
particulars, 50
parties, 34
party, 34
pass, 18
passes, 5
past, 33
past-due, 33
pasted, 20
pasture, 10
patent, 31
patient, 8
pattern, 32
pay, 6
pay roll, 6
payable, 23
payment, 23
pays, 2
peculiar, 19
penalty, 29
pencil, 18
pending, 26
people, 2
per, 23
per cent, 23
percentage, 23
perfect, 33
perfectly, 33
perforated, 23
perhaps, 23
period, 22
periodical, 25
periodically, 25
permanent, 23
permission, 41
permit, 23
permitted, 23
perpetual, 23
perplexing, 23
person, 23
personal, 23
personality, 29
personally, 23
personnel, 23
persons, 23
persuade, 23
persuaded, 23
persuasion, 23
pertaining, 31
petition, 41
phase, 1
philosophy, 41
phone, 1
phoned, 21
physical, 25
physician, 8
physiology, 40
piano, 11
pick, 6
picture, 10
pictures, 18
piece, 18
pig, 6

pigs, 18
pin, 6
pink, 16
pins, 18
pipes, 18
Pittsfield, 52
Pittsburgh, 52
place, 2
places, 5
plain, 6,
Plainfield, 52
plan, 6
planned, 21
plans, 18
plant, 21
planted, 21
plate, 6
Plattsburg, 52
pleadings, 49
pleasant, 21
please, 9
pleased, 9
pleasing, 9
pleasure, 18
pledge, 3
plenty, 21
plow, 19
plug, 13
plumbing, 16
plus, 13
pocket, 4
poems, 11
poetry, 11
poets, 11
point, 21
poison, 10
pole, 6
policy, 6
polish, 6
political, 25
politics, 6
pool, 13
poor, 13
popular, 4
population, 50
porch, 6
port, 32
portable, 32
portfolio, 32
portion, 8
ports, 32
position, 47
positive, 26
positively, 26
possession, 8
possibilities, 29
possible, 23
possibly, 9
post, 18
post card, 35
postage, 35
post office, 35
postal, 35
postdate, 35
posted, 20
posthaste, 35
postmark, 35
postmaster, 35
postpaid, 35
postpone, 35
postponed, 35
postscript, 35
pound, 34
pounds, 34
powder, 19
power, 19
powerful, 29
practical, 25
practically, 25
practice, 18
precaution, 8

precedent, 31
predict, 33
prefer, 6
preferred, 17
preliminary, 41
premises, 5
premium, 22
preparation, 8
prepare, 2
prepared, 17
prescription, 8
presence, 34
present, 34
presented, 34
president, 31
presses, 5
pressure, 18
presumably, 50
presume, 50
presumed, 50
presumptive, 50
prettiest, 33
pretty, 6
prevent, 21
prevented, 21
prevention, 8
previous, 22
previously, 22
prices, 5
Princeton, 53
principal, 18
principally, 9
printer, 21
prior, 11
private, 6
privilege, 41
privileged, 41
privileges, 41
probable, 34
probably, 34
probate, 23
problem, 23
procedure, 23
proceed, 23
proceedings, 49
process, 23
processes, 23
procure, 18
produce, 22
produced, 22
producers, 22
produces, 22
product, 33
production, 13
productive, 33
professional, 23
professor, 23
profit, 23
profitable, 23
profitably, 23
program, 29
progress, 26
progressive, 26
prohibit, 23
project, 33
prominence, 20
prominent, 21
promise, 23
promised, 23
promises, 23
promote, 23
promotion, 23
prompt, 21
promptly, 21
promptness, 21
proof, 23
proper, 23
properly, 23
property, 26
proportion, 23
proportionate, 23
proposal, 47

proposed, 47
proposes, 47
proposition, 47
propositions, 47
proprietor, 23
propriety, 40
prosecute, 52
prosecution, 52
prospect, 33
prospective, 33
prosperity, 29
prosperous, 23
protect, 33
protected, 33
protection, 8
protest, 33
protested, 33
proud, 19
prove, 23
proved, 23
proven, 23
provide, 23
provided, 23
provision, 23
prune, 13
psychological, 40
psychology, 40
public, 45
publication, 45
publications, 45
publish, 45
published, 45
publishers, 45
pull, 13
pulled, 17
pump, 16
punch, 16
purchase, 32
purchased, 32
purchases, 32
purchasing, 32
pure, 19
purloin, 23
purple, 23
purpose, 26
purposes, 26
pursuant, 23
pursue, 23
pursued, 23
pursuit, 23
push, 13
put, 4
qualifications, 29
qualities, 29
quantities, 45
quantity, 45
quart, 32
quarter, 32
quarterly, 32
queen, 15
query, 15
question, 49
questions, 49
quick, 15
quicker, 15
quickest, 33
quiet, 15
quit, 15
quite, 15
quota, 15
quotation, 41
quote, 15
quoted, 20
radiation, 11
radiator, 11
radical, 25
radio, 11
radius, 22
rag, 6
railroad, 51
railroads, 51
railway, 15

raise, 18
ran, 6
random, 31
range, 2
rapid, 6
rapidly, 9
rarely, 9
rate, 1
rated, 20
rates, 18
rather, 14
ratification, 29
ratify, 29
ration, 8
raw, 4
reach, 6
reached, 2
reaches, 18
read, 6
reader, 1
readers, 2
readily, 9
ready, 6
real, 1
realize, 18
reappear, 12
reason, 10
reasonable, 23
reasonably, 10
reasons, 12
rebate, 12
recent, 21
recall, 6
receipt, 12
receive, 12
reception, 12
rechecked, 12
reciprocate, 39
recitation, 41
reclaim, 12
recline, 12
recognize, 12
recognized, 51
recommend, 34
recommendation, 41
recommended, 34
reconcile, 37
reconstruction, 37
record, 17
redemption, 31
reduce, 22
reduced, 22
reduces, 22
reduction, 13
refer, 51,
reference, 51
referred, 51
referring, 51
refers, 51
refining, 12
reflect, 33
reflected, 33
refund, 21
refusal, 39
refused, 39
refuses, 39
regain, 12
regard, 49
regards, 49
region, 10
register, 10
registered, 17
regret, 6
regular, 45
regularly, 45
reimburse, 37
reimbursed, 37
reimbursement, 37
rejected, 33
related, 20
relation, 8
relationship, 25

relative, 26
relay, 1
release, 18
releases, 5
reliability, 29
reliable, 23
religious, 18
reluctant, 41
rely, 2
remain, 20
remainder, 52
remained, 20
remake, 12
remedy, 6
remember, 34
remind, 34
reminded, 34
remit, 17
remittance, 17
remittances, 17
remitted, 17
remodeling, 4
remove, 18
rename, 12
render, 21
rendered, 21
renew, 22
renewal, 22
renewed, 22
rent, 21
rental, 21
rented, 21
repair, 12
repaired, 17
repeat, 12
repeated, 20
repeatedly, 20
repetition, 41
replace, 12
replacement, 23
replied, 12
report, 32
reported, 32
reports, 32
represent, 34
representative, 34
represented, 34
represents, 34
reproduction, 13
reputation, 41
request, 46
requested, 46
requests, 46
require, 40
required, 40
requirements, 40
requisition, 15
resale, 10
research, 10
reservation, 12
reserve, 12
reserved, 12
reservoir, 15
residence, 31
resident, 31
resist, 33
resistance, 33
resort, 32
resources, 12
respect, 33
respectfully, 33
respectively, 33
respondent, 26
response, 12
responsibility, 29
responsible, 23
rest, 33
rested, 33
resting, 33
restitution, 40
rests, 33

result, 38
resulted, 38
resulting, 38
results, 38
resume, 50
resumed, 50
retail, 1
retain, 31
retained, 31
retake, 12
retention, 31
retired, 17
retribution, 40
return, 16
returned, 16
reveal, 12
revenue, 22
reverse, 12
review, 19
reviews, 19
revise, 12
revision, 12
reward, 38
rid, 6
right, 7
rights, 7
ring, 16
rise, 2
risk, 18
river, 3
road, 1
roadway, 15
rob, 4
rock, 4
Rockford, 53
rod, 4
rolled, 17
roller, 6
romance, 20
roof, 13
room, 13
root, 13
ropes, 18
rose, 18
rotten, 31
rough, 13
round, 23
route, 13
routed, 20
routine, 13
royal, 10
royalty, 29
rub, 13
rubber, 13
rule, 13
run, 16
runner, 16
runs, 16
rush, 16
rushed, 16
rushing, 16
sacrifice, 18
sad, 18
safe, 1
safety, 18
said, 18
sake, 2
salable, 23
salary, 18
sales, 18
salesman, 18
salesmen, 20
salt, 6
same, 1
sample, 3
sanction, 16
sand, 21
sane, 1
sash, 18
satin, 31
satisfaction, 16

satisfactorily, 16
satisfactory, 16
satisfied, 16
satisfy, 16
Saturday, 22
save, 1
saved, 1
savings, 49
saw, 4
say, 1
says, 5
scandals, 21
scene, 1
schedules, 10
scheduling, 18
scheme, 18
scholarship, 25
school, 13
science, 11
scientific, 26
score, 18
scrap, 18
screw, 13
sea, 1
seaboard, 17
sealed, 17
search, 3
season, 1
seat, 1
seats, 18
second, 21
secondary, 21
secretary, 18
section, 8
sectional, 8
secure, 18
securities, 29
security, 29
sedan, 18
see, 1
seed, 1
seemed, 21
seemingly, 49
seems, 2
seen, 1
sees, 1
seethe, 18
seldom, 31
select, 33
selected, 33
selection, 8
self-contained, 47
self-defense, 47
self-educated, 47
self-made, 47
self-pity, 47
self-sacrifice, 47
self-satisfied, 47
self-styled, 47
self-supporting, 47
seller, 3
sells, 18
semester, 18
semiannual, 10
send, 14
sense, 18
sensibilities, 29
sent, 21
sentence, 31
separate, 18
separated, 20
separately, 9
September, 22
series, 18
serious, 22
seriously, 22
serve, 3
service, 18
services, 5
servings, 49
session, 8

set, 18
settle, 3
settled, 17
settlement, 23
several, 20
sew, 1
shade, 2
shades, 18
shall, 4
shape, 6
shaped, 2
share, 6
shares, 2
sharp, 6
she, 6
sheep, 2
sheets, 18
shell, 6
shelves, 18
shingle, 16
ship, 4
shipmate, 27
shipment, 23
shipped, 8
shipshape, 27
shipwreck, 27
shoe, 13
shoes, 18
shop, 4
short, 27
shortage, 27
shortages, 27
shorten, 27
shorter, 27
shortest, 33
shortly, 27
should, 9
shoulder, 17
shovels, 13
show, 2
shown, 6
shows, 18
shrinkage, 16
sickness, 18
sides, 11
siege, 18
sign, 18
signature, 18
signed, 21
silent, 21
similar, 3
simple, 18
simply, 9
since, 18
sincere, 18
sincerely, 9
sing, 16
single, 16
sink, 16
sister, 5
situated, 22
situation, 45
sizes, 5
sketch, 18
slight, 2
slightest, 33
slightly, 9
slowest, 33
slowly, 9
small, 6
smoke, 18
smooth, 18
snap, 18
snow, 1
snowy, 11
so, 1
soap, 18
social, 8
society, 40
soft, 4
soil, 10

122

soiled, 17
sold, 17
solicit, 6
solicitation, 41
solicited, 20
solid, 6
solve, 6
some, 16
somebody, 44
someone, 44
something, 16
sometime, 32
sometimes, 32
somewhere, 44
son, 16
song, 16
soon, 19
sooner, 19
sorrow, 6
sort, 32
sound, 23
source, 6
sources, 5
south, 19
southeast, 19
southeastern, 32
southern, 32
southwestern, 32
space, 18
spaces, 5
spare, 6
speak, 26
speaks, 26
special, 8
specific, 18
specifications, 29
specified, 29
specify, 29
speculation, 50
speed, 18
spend, 26
spent, 26
spirit, 18
splendid, 21
spoiled, 17
spoke, 18
spoon, 13
sport, 32
sports, 32
spot, 4
spread, 18
spring, 16
Springfield, 52
square, 15
staff, 18
stain, 1,
Stamford, 53
stamp, 18
stand, 32
standard, 31
standing, 32
standpoint, 32
stands, 32
star, 3
start, 18
started, 20
starts, 3
state, 45
stated, 45
statement, 45
states, 45
station, 41
stationed, 41
stationery, 41
statistical, 25
statistics, 18
status, 13
stay, 1
stayed, 1
steadily, 20
steady, 20

steal, 1
steam, 1
steamship, 25
stenographer, 31
stenographic, 31
step, 18
still, 18
stimulate, 50
stimulated, 50
stimulates, 50
stock, 4
stomach, 31
stone, 6
stood, 13
stop, 4
storage, 2
store, 6
stored, 17
storm, 6
story, 6
stove, 1
stow, 1
straighten, 31
straightened, 31
street, 26
streets, 26
strength, 16
strictly, 33
string, 16
strong, 16
strongly, 16
structural, 18
structure, 18
stub, 13
student, 31
studied, 20
studies, 20
study, 20
stuff, 13
style, 18
styles, 2
subchief, 38
subdivision, 38
subeditor, 38
subhead, 38
subject, 50
sublet, 38
submit, 38
submitted, 38
subordinate, 38
subscribe, 38
subscriber, 38
subscription, 38
subsequent, 40
substance, 38
substantial, 38
substantiate, 38
substitute, 40
substitution, 40
subtracted, 38
subway, 38
success, 50
successes, 50
such, 26
suction, 13
sudden, 31
suffer, 13
suffered, 17
sufficient, 13
sugar, 13
suggest, 20
suggested, 20
suggestion, 20
suit, 22
suitable, 23
suited, 22
sum, 16
summary, 16
summer, 16
summons, 20
sun, 16

Sunday, 22
superb, 35
superficially, 35
superintendent, 37
superior, 35
supervision, 35
supervisor, 35
supplement, 23
supplemental, 23
supplementary, 23
supplied, 18
support, 35
supports, 35
suppose, 47
supposed, 47
supposition, 47
supremacy, 35
supreme, 35
sure, 18
surely, 18
surety, 29
surgical, 25
surprise, 18
surrender, 21
surrendered, 21
surrounding, 23
suspended, 26
suspension, 41
sustained, 31
swam, 13
swear, 13
sweater, 13
sweet, 13
swell, 13
swing, 16
switch, 13
swivel, 13
swollen, 13
sworn, 13
syndicate, 39
system, 31
table, 23
tabulation, 50
tags, 18
take, 6
taken, 2
talent, 21
talked, 4
tank, 16
Tarrytown, 53
task, 18
taught, 4
tax, 5
taxation, 8
taxed, 5
taxes, 5
taxicab, 5
tea, 1
teacher, 6
teachers, 18
team, 1
technical, 25
technology, 40
teeth, 6
telegram, 29
telegrams, 29
telegraph, 6
telephone, 6
tell, 6
temper, 31
temperature, 31
temple, 31
temporarily, 31
temporary, 31
tenant, 31
tend, 31
tendency, 31
tender, 31
tendered, 31
tent, 31
tentative, 31

term, 32
termed, 32
terminal, 32
terminate, 32
terminology, 40
terms, 32
territory, 6
test, 33
tested, 33
testify, 29
tests, 33
text, 5
textile, 5
than, 9
thank, 17
Thanksgiving, 44
that, 7
the, 3
theater, 6
their, 4
them, 7
theme, 6
themselves, 25
then, 9
theory, 22
there, 4
thereby, 4
therefore, 4
therein, 4
thereon, 6
thermometer, 32
these, 18
they, 9
thick, 3
thicker, 6
thickness, 3
thin, 6
thing, 14
things, 49
think, 14
thinner, 3
third, 17
this, 14
thorough, 6
thoroughly, 9
those, 19
though, 6
thought, 6
thoughtful, 29
thread, 6
three, 6
throat, 3
through, 13
throughout, 49
throw, 6
thrown, 6
Thursday, 22
thus, 13
tickets, 18
tie, 6,
tied, 6
timber, 31
time, 32
times, 32
tip, 6
tire, 2
tired, 17
title, 6
to, 7
today, 20
toe, 1
together, 14
told, 17
tomatoes, 31
tomorrow, 31
ton, 16
tone, 6
tongue, 16
tonight, 31
tonnage, 16
tonsillitis, 40

123

took, 13
tool, 13
tooth, 13
top, 4
torch, 6
tore, 6
torn, 6
Torrington, 53
total, 1
totally, 9
touch, 16
tough, 13
tour, 13
toward, 17
towels, 19
tower, 19
town, 23
township, 25
toy, 10
tracer, 18
track, 6
tract, 33
tractor, 33
trade, 1
trading, 3
traffic, 6
trained, 21
transact, 35
transaction, 35
transcribe, 35
transcript, 35
transfer, 35
transferred, 35
transfers, 35
transit, 35
transition, 35
translated, 35
translation, 35
transmission, 41
transmit, 35
transmittal, 35
transmitted, 35
transparent, 35
transportation, 41
transposition, 47
travel, 6
treasurer, 18
treasury, 18
treat, 1
treated, 20
treatment, 23
tremendous, 20
trend, 21
trial, 11
tribune, 19
tried, 2
trimmed, 21
trip, 6
trips, 18
trouble, 23
truck, 13
true, 13
trunk, 16
trust, 13
tub, 13
tube, 19
Tuesday, 22
turn, 32
turned, 32
twice, 15
twin, 15
type, 2
typical, 25
typographical, 25
ultimate, 38
unable, 20
unaccountable, 23
uncertain, 37
unclaimed, 37
uncle, 16
uncompromising, 47

uncontrollable, 47
undecided, 37
under, 17
undercharges, 17
undersized, 17
understand, 32
understandable, 32
understood, 17
undoubtedly, 37
unduly, 37
unearned, 21
unenterprising, 47
uneven, 13
unfair, 37
unfilled, 37
unfortunate, 38
uninsured, 47
union, 22
unique, 19
unit, 19
unite, 19
united, 20
unjust, 37
unknowingly, 49
unknown, 37
unless, 51
unloaded, 37
unnecessary, 37
unnoticed, 37
unobtainable, 31
unpacked, 37
unpaid, 37
unreasonable, 37
unsatisfactory, 37
unsettled, 37
until, 37
unusually, 20
up, 13
upon, 26
upper, 13
upward, 38
urge, 3
urgent, 26
urgently, 26
us, 18
use, 19
used, 19
useful, 19
usefulness, 29
uselessly, 51
usual, 20
utilization, 19
utterly, 13
vacancies, 18
vacant, 21
vacation, 8
vacuum, 22
vain, 1
valuation, 49
value, 49
valued, 49
variation, 11
variety, 40
various, 22
vase, 1
vast, 18
vault, 6
venture, 21
verification, 29
verify, 29
versus, 5
very, 14
via, 11
vicinity, 18
view, 19
views, 19
violation, 11
virtually, 18
visit, 18
visited, 20

visual, 18
vital, 2
voice, 10
void, 10
volume, 22
vote, 1
voucher, 19
wages, 13
wagon, 13
waist, 13
wait, 13
waited, 20
waiver, 13
walk, 13
wall, 13
walnut, 13
want, 21
wanted, 21
war, 13
warehouse, 50
warm, 13
warrant, 21
warranted, 21
was, 9
wash, 13
washer, 13
Washington, 53
waste, 13
wasted, 20
watch, 13
water, 13
wave, 13
way, 13
ways, 13
we, 13
weak, 20
wear, 13
wears, 13
weather, 14
Wednesday, 22
week, 20
weekly, 20
weigh, 13
weighed, 13
weight, 13
welcome, 16
well, 3
went, 21
were, 7
west, 13
western, 32
Westport, 52
wet, 13
whale, 13
what, 11
whatever, 19
whatsoever, 44
wheat, 13
wheel, 13
when, 9
whenever, 19
whensoever, 44
where, 17
whereabouts, 17
whereas, 17
wherein, 17
wheresoever, 44
wherever, 19
whether, 14
which, 4
while, 13
whole, 13
wholesale, 6
winter, 21
whip, 13
white, 13
who, 13
wholesale, 18
whom, 13
whomsoever, 44

whose, 18
whosoever, 44
why, 32
wide, 13
width, 13
wife, 13
will, 3
wills, 3
Wilmington, 53
win, 13
wind, 21
Winfield, 52
wire, 13
wired, 17
wires, 13
wise, 13
wish, 20
wished, 20
with, 4
withdrew, 13
within, 44
without, 19
withstand, 44
witness, 13
wives, 13
woe, 13
woman, 20
women, 20
won, 19
wonder, 51
wondering, 51
won't, 21
wood, 13
wooden, 31
wool, 13
woolen, 13
word, 17
work, 16
worked, 16
world, 20
worn, 13
worries, 13
worse, 13
worst, 13
worth, 14
worthless, 51
worthy, 14
would, 3
woven, 13
wrenches, 18
write, 7
writer, 8
writers, 8
written, 31
wrong, 16
wrote, 1
yacht, 15
yard, 17
yarn, 15
yarns, 15
year, 7
years, 7
yeast, 15
yell, 15
yellow, 15
yes, 15
yesterday, 51
yet, 16
yield, 17
yoke, 15
you, 7
young, 16
your, 7
yours, 7
yourself, 25
yourselves, 25
Yours truly, 7
youth, 15
Zanesville, 52
zone, 1

124

CPSIA information can be obtained
at www.ICGtesting.com
Printed in the USA
BVHW032010261122
652660BV00008B/626

9 781163 146972